Almost Home

Almost Home

◆

My Life Story

Vol 1

Damien Echols

iUniverse, Inc.
New York Lincoln Shanghai

Almost Home
My Life Story

iUniverse books may be ordered through booksellers or by contacting:

iUniverse
2021 Pine Lake Road, Suite 100
Lincoln, NE 68512
www.iuniverse.com
1-800-Authors (1-800-288-4677)

ISBN-13: 978-0-595-35701-7 (pbk)
ISBN-13: 978-0-595-80178-7 (ebk)
ISBN-10: 0-595-35701-6 (pbk)
ISBN-10: 0-595-80178-1 (ebk)

Printed in the United States of America

Contents

Foreword

The first time HBO aired the documentary "Paradise Lost—The Child Murders of Robin Hood Hills," I was living in the Hollywood Hills, miles and a millennium away from stories like these. There is a certain lurid fascination I have always had with crime and criminals, and I had recently found a home in the City of Broken Dreams, where the Manson Family and the Black Dahlia ruled the sickly jaded pop culture of Los Angeles in the early 90s. I had not been prepared for the tragic tale of these boys, who are now referred to as the West Memphis Three.

Filmmakers Joe Berlinger and Bruce Sinofsky did an incredibly balanced portrayal of the trial and conviction of Damien Echols, Jason Baldwin and Jesse Misskelley. The documentary commented neither on the possible innocence or guilt of the three, who were tried as adults for the heinous murders of three younger boys, Christopher Byers, Steven Branch and Michael Moore. Berlinger and Sinofsky did what great documentary filmmakers do, document. They shot, kept shooting, kept eyes on all who were involved in a case that was obviously incredibly doomed from the start.

No evidence linked the West Memphis Three to the murders, besides an admission of guilt by Jesse Misskelley (who possesses an IQ level of 73), forced out of him after twelve consecutive hours of questioning, with only the last forty five minutes put on tape. It was more a fabricated rendition of what the law officers wanted to believe happened that terrible day in Arkansas, than a confession. It was something to appease the local community, locked in a "Satanic Panic" like a scene out of "The Crucible," a vigilante mob looking for a witch to burn, who wanted justice even if that justice was actually unjust. This pitiful piece of "evidence" was enough to convict all three of capital murder and resulted in life sentences for Jesse and Jason, and death by lethal injection for Damien Echols, scheduled for the year 2000.

I was outraged. Yet, it seemed as if the documentary would have been enough to exonerate these kids. The truth was blatantly there, on the screen, and couldn't be denied. I thought the justice system would soon undo its wrongs, because I believed in America then, so much more than I do now. My roommate made me a prayer box, with a photograph of the still adolescent Damien on a string inside.

Later, I found a large paperback that formed a kind of yearbook for all the death row inmates in America awaiting execution. Damien's photograph and name were in the book, now almost two years after the case had gone to trial. Then, the second documentary "Paradise Lost II: Revelations" aired on HBO. This film focused on the wake of the convictions, the formation of Free the West Memphis Three organization by Burk Sauls, Kathy Bakken and Grove Pashley, the system of appeals the now young men were facing, their reflections on their unjust sentencing and the incredulousness of the different groups of people who identified with the WM3. It seemed that having long black hair, a love of heavy metal music and a tendency toward esoteric reading could get you the death penalty, and the backlash was starting mobilize.

The sequel also carefully studied the idiosyncratic and suspicious behavior of Mark Byers, stepfather of one of the slain boys, whose wife had died mysteriously after the trial, and who was accused later of forcing two young boys to fight each other and abusing another family's child. Byers is currently serving time in prison for a number of other unrelated offenses. After viewing this film, I still somehow believed that the justice system would correct itself, that the movement to free the innocent was enough and that America would do right by the law. I thought possibly a third documentary would be in pre-production, one that would be about the day the WM3 would walk out of prison, no longer incarcerated by an intolerant and ridiculous court that could let the real killer go free, thinking that convenient scapegoats (who did not have the funds for proper legal representation, let alone costly forensic testing) would be enough to appease not only the community of West Memphis, but justice itself.

The third film is starting production. The Berlinger-Sinofsky team has gone on to make a documentary about Metallica, who generously donated their music to Paradise I & II, and hopefully III, and two feature films are in pre-production about the WM3. The website WM3.org flourishes, and celebrities like Eddie Vedder and Winona Ryder have championed the cause with speeches and considerable financial donations. Many articles, essays, compendiums, and books, including the definitive "The Devil's Knot," by Mara Leveritt, have been written on this compelling and disgraceful miscarriage of justice, about the discrimination of those who are "different" in a community where conformity is law and far more restrictive than anything that is on the books.

More than a decade after learning about this travesty, I decided to write to Damien Echols. I made a donation to his defense fund, and bought him some books from his Amazon wish list. He wrote back to thank me, and asked if I was a comedian. I said that I was, and that I had been following the case for many years, and could not understand why he was still on death row.

We became fast friends. I wanted to know how he was doing, how he survived, how he could still retain a sense of humor and continue to develop as a human being in such a desperate climate. He granted me an interview on my website, and we now regularly have dialogues from his cell on death row. His words are read by countless people around the world, typed into my computer, from his tiny, elegant script, always on long, yellow legal pads. It is humbling, for he has never seen the internet.

I realize that I take so much for granted, like life, for instance. Some have not that luxury. I imagine that being on death row is like having a terminal disease, and the race to find a cure is running alongside you, sometimes fast, or slow, depending on whatever else is happening. You gain, you lose. Momentum is both your savior and your nemesis. How does one live with that?

We write to each other on an almost daily basis. It is all merely my questions, and his answers. I wanted to hear more, because his story has been told by so many, but not yet by him. His story is far more than a gross miscarriage of justice, but a tale of uncommon wisdom and redemption, faith and love, forgiveness and a diverse passion for Wagner and hair bands like Kixx and Skid Row.

Damien Echols is a holy man, as well as a complex, hilarious, erudite, brilliant, forthright, seeker of knowledge and truth. He also secretly loves pro-wrestling! His capacity for understanding and tolerance run deeper than any other "guru how-to" I have ever spent my self help money on. He and his wife, Lorri Davis, have become sort of a surrogate family for me. Their bond is tremendously loving, and they remind me of my husband and myself. We are a mirror image, although their reflection is distorted by injustice and the reversal that in his case, Damien was guilty before being allowed to be proven innocent. If we are the land of the free, the West Memphis Three must be released. They are political prisoners, and until they are free, none of us are free.

Damien Echols is the Heavy Metal Dalai Lama, the Nelson Mandela of Rock and Roll, the Deepak Chopra of Death Row. He keeps equanimity and compassion in a place where most would have lost their minds and so many have already lost their lives. His spiritual practice is inspiring in its ability to allow him to cope with what would be literally hell for everyone else. He has become my teacher. Allow him to become yours.

Freedom, justice and love will prevail.

Margaret Cho
May, 2004

Preface

The purpose of an introduction is to take two people who have never met, and formally induce a culturally acceptable greeting between them. Maybe we do this so that the two people can then be acquainted, and possibly become friends with one another thus connecting the dots in our circle of friends, or maybe we do it because we feel like the two people we're introducing to each other might learn something valuable from their new acquaintance. Learning something valuable is usually good, and by introducing you to this book by my friend Damien Echols, I'm satisfied that you'll agree with me about the value of it.

The life story in this book isn't your average autobiography; in many ways it's *more* average than the average autobiography. Damien hasn't fought in any wars or discovered any important scientific principles. He hasn't traveled much, and he's never been a millionaire or a movie star. He hasn't lived a life full of adventure or conquest, but the drama of his life is an important one to read and know about, because Damien represents a lot of people living here in the Land of the Free. You know people like him.

Growing up, he didn't have much use for conformity. He was never one to take on the appearance, beliefs, likes or dislikes of his peers in that way that so many teenagers are driven to. "Fitting In" never held much water for him. He grew up with the courage to be himself, and trust me, in a violent, judgmental, and territorial place like an American High School, it takes courage to even carry around a book that nobody else has. That's nothing new or ground-breaking, though. Simply being an outcast doesn't make much of a story all by itself. There are lots of kids out there who dress different, read books that they discovered on their own, or think outside the militantly rigid and violently maintained borders of whatever teenager society they happen to find themselves a citizen of.

The fact that there's lots of outcasts makes Damien's story even more important and disturbing. If he was not on death row in an Arkansas prison, his story might not be all that different from many other outcast's. Damien, however, is a victim of a type of panic that's been a part of human nature since we've been using language. This sometimes hysterically defended belief that "different is bad" goes way back, and clearly it's still an idea that rules the world.

The state of Arkansas wants very badly to execute Damien, but even a cursory look at his case tells the rational among us that he, along with Jason Baldwin and Jessie Misskelley, are innocent of the crime they've been locked up for. The three of them have come to be known as The West Memphis Three, and their cause has been embraced by people all over the world who see it for what it is—an example of how ordinary people can become victims of a system that is supposed to protect and serve us.

The fact that Damien is on death row puts a big red circle around his autobiography. Is it a warning? Is he telling us what not to do to avoid his unfair fate? I can tell you by way of introduction that the young man you are about to meet is certainly a standout among average outcasts. He's everyone and no one at the same time; a part of our world, but locked away from it and us in a nine by twelve cell.

Damien is a very disciplined man, impressive in his ability to turn his situation around and create something positive and productive from it. He reads constantly, and has carefully and methodically transformed himself into a writer. This book is poignant and disturbing, full of focused observations and insight that, in some ways, explain why he's in that cell.

There are some people who think people like Damien are evil simply because they're not easy to define or categorize. Damien lived proudly outside of their boundaries, so when something horrible happened in their town, they looked beyond what they understood and felt comfortable with and saw Damien standing there. They couldn't look deeper because they couldn't see any deeper. They'd been conditioned by the "different is bad" rule.

Damien has been my friend since the moment I realized what had happened to him. Like a lot of people, I see a little of myself in him. I grew up hearing "be yourself" and learning that individuality was important. My favorite people have always been distinctly individualistic, and Damien is one of them. Those of us who know him have learned a lot about perseverance and strength in the face of unfairness. Damien, Jason and Jessie haven't allowed the Arkansas Department of Corrections to turn them into criminals or even convicts. They all seem to exist outside of the prison system they've been trapped in for over a decade, and they've wisely used their experience to make themselves better and stronger.

Damien's autobiography shows us a young man who still doesn't conform, even in the most rigidly conformist environment imaginable. He's still the same person he was before he was arrested, just a decade older and perhaps more informed about the roots of unfairness and injustice. This book is his from start to finish. Nobody is editing him or putting words into his mouth. No newscaster is spinning rumors into a sordid tale to tease you into staying though the commercials, and nobody is interpreting or claiming to know what he "really means" by whatever he's saying. This book is sad and funny, heartbreaking and honest, but it isn't a whiny "look what they've done to me" tirade against the forces that put him where he is.

Damien isn't a complainer. He isn't a murderer. He isn't a symbol or a metaphor. He's not a martyr or a saint. He's precisely and exactly Damien Echols.

—Burk Sauls, August, 2004

Introduction

Writing down your life's experiences can be very rewarding. I find that when I start telling someone a story it isn't long before their eyes glaze over and they begin thinking about earwigs and whirling dervishes. The whole world has ADD, and no one has the time to listen to a story that lasts longer than thirty seconds. Ah, but once you begin compiling those stories into a book, people become completely absorbed. Their attention is riveted to the page. I thrive on that.

Some of the stories in this book are things I've wanted to tell someone for years, but I was never given the chance or excuse to do so. When I first began communicating with Margaret Cho, my excuse was born. Without her, this book would have never happened. Every single day, I hopped out of bed, grabbed my pen, and started writing. I didn't stop until lights out every night. Some days, after writing for eighteen hours straight, my fingers refused to grip the pen and my wrist throbbed in agony. Still, I couldn't stop. The story continued to spill out of me and I could not rest until I captured the words on paper. This book is in reality one long letter to Margaret. I was driven to get it all out.

This book also serves as an exorcism of sorts for me. My life abruptly changed course in 1993. The world I knew came to an end through no fault of my own. Everyone and everything I knew became a ghost that haunted the inside of my head. With this book I laid my past to rest. Now I feel like I'm free to move on and begin a new chapter. All my friends and lovers dissolved like a spoonful of sugar in a glass of water.

Ever since the age of fourteen I've wanted to write a book, but was always uncertain about what to write. So, I wrote about what I knew. What will make me happy is if you not only read this book, but feel it. I want you to walk through these pages next to me. Hurt when I hurt, laugh when I laugh, and love when I love. This is an invitation to walk a mile in my shoes. That's what all good stories do, in my opinion.

What are you waiting for? Take my hand, and we'll be off.

Damien Echols
6–28–04
10:19 pm

I

My name is Damien Echols, although it wasn't always so. At birth I was different in both name and essence. On December 11, 1974, when I came into the world, I was given the name Michael Hutchison at the insistence of my father. My mother had a different name in mind, but my father would hear none of it.

The hospital I was born in still stands in the small rundown town of West Memphis, Arkansas. It's the same hospital my grandmother died in twenty years later. As a child I was jealous of my sister who had the privilege of being born two years later across the bridge in Memphis, Tennessee. In my youth Memphis always felt like home to me. When we crossed the bridge into Tennessee I had the sensation of being where I belonged, and thought it only fair that I should have been the one born there. After all, my sister didn't even care where she was born.

My mother and grandmother were both fascinated by the fact that when the doctor cleared my mother to go home, I was placed in a Christmas stocking. They kept the stocking for many years, and I had to hear the story often. I found out later that hospitals all over the country do the same thing for every baby born in the month of December, but this fact seemed to be lost on my mother, and it marked the beginning of a lifetime of denial. After saving the stocking as if it were a valuable family heirloom for seventeen years, it was unceremoniously left behind in a move that was less than well-planned.

Other than the stocking, I had only one memento saved from childhood—a pillow. My grandmother gave it to me the day I left the hospital, and I slept on it until I was about seventeen years old, when it was left behind in the same ill-fated move. I could never sleep without that pillow as a child; it was my security blanket. By the end it was nothing more than a ball of stuffing housed in a pillowcase that was rapidly disintegrating.

I was born in the winter and was a child of the winter. I was only truly happy when the days were short, the nights were long, and my teeth were chattering. I love the winter. Every year I long for it, look forward to it, even though I always feel as if it's turning me inside out. The beauty and loneliness of it hurts my heart and carries with it all the memories of every winter before. Even now, after having been locked in a cell for ten years, at the coming of winter I can still close my eyes and feel myself walking the streets as everyone else lies in bed asleep. I remember how the ice sounded as it cracked in the trees every time the wind blew. Sometimes I was so cold that I wanted to cry, but still did not want to go indoors and miss the magick of it. The air could be so cold that it scoured my throat with each breath, but it was beautiful. There's a tremendous amount of emotional pain that comes with the magick and beauty of winter, but I still mourn when the season ends, like I'm losing my best friend.

The first true memories I have of my life are of being with my grandmother. We lived in a small mobile home trailer in Senatobia, Mississippi. I remember the purple and white trailer sitting on top of a hill covered with pine trees. We had two large black dogs named Smokey and Bear, which we had raised from puppies. One of my earliest memories was of hearing the dogs barking and lunging against their chains like madmen as my grandmother stood in the backyard with a pistol, shooting at a poisonous snake. She didn't stop shooting, even as the snake slithered it's way under the huge propane tank in the backyard. Only in hindsight, years later, did I realize she would have blown us all straight to hell if she would have hit the tank. At the time I was so young that I viewed the entire scene with nothing but extreme curiosity. It was the first time I had ever seen a snake, and it was combined with the additional spectacle of my grandmother charging out the back door, blazing away like a gunslinger.

My grandmother worked as a cashier at a truck stop, so during the day I had to stay at a day care center. I can only remember it because it was horrific. I remember being dropped off so early in the morning that it was still dark, and led to a room in which other children were sleeping on cots. I was given a cot and told that I should take a nap until "Captain Kangaroo" (my favorite television show) came on. The problem was that I could not, under any circumstances, go to sleep without my pillow/security blanket. The very thought hurt me, filled me with an overwhelming sense of cold dread, and I felt abandoned and alone. I began to scream and cry at the top of my lungs, tears running down my face. It awakened and frightened every other child in the dark room, so that within a few seconds, everyone was crying and screaming while frantic day care workers ran from cot to cot in an attempt to find out what was wrong. By the time they got everyone quiet and dried all the tears it was time for Captain Kangaroo and I was quickly absorbed into the epic saga of Mr. Green Jeans and a puppet moose who lived life in perpetual fear of being pelted with a storm of ping-pong balls. After the first day, my grandmother never forgot to send my pillow with me.

She also brought me small surprises home from work, one of which was a plastic fireman's hat that became my most prized possession. All of the boys and most of the girls in the day care center had them, so everyone's name had to be written inside their hat with a black marker in order to prevent confusion. Mine said "Michael H." Never Mike, always Michael. I don't believe that anyone ever called me Mike, although every other child named Michael was always Mike. I was frequently asked after my name was changed if it was odd having grown accustomed to being called by a different name. The answer is no, and the reason is because I was never Michael Hutchison. That was someone else, someone that ceased to exist long ago. I have always been Damien Echols. At first, every great once in a while, someone who wanted to pretend they knew me better than they truly did would try to address me otherwise. I usually look upon them with contempt.

The only other memory I have of that time is of my mother and father coming for a visit. My sister was just an infant, and I can still see my mother sitting in the dark living room holding her, rocking her to sleep. I went outside and sat on what my grandmother called a "Big wheel." It's like a tough plastic tricycle, only laid back like a chopper and much cooler. My legs were too short to reach the pedals, so I just sat there. Suddenly my father came around the corner and stopped when he saw me. I should have known to run when I saw the demented gleam in his eyes.

Just for the record, my biological father is a lunatic. He is without question insane. When I say that my father suffers from madness, I mean it in the absolute best of ways. He used to make me laugh until I was hurting. His dementia only endeared him to me even more, and I believe I inherited almost all of my sense of humor from him. Some say that's not a good thing.

When he saw me sitting on the Big Wheel, he cocked his head to the side and studied me like a bird of ill intent before asking, "Want a push?" I had my reservations when I saw the look of glee on his face, but I couldn't very well give up a free ride—after all, there's no telling when another would come along. I reluctantly nodded my head, and a grin spread across his face, full of teeth that seemed far too large and numerous. My father could be cleaned up to look presentable for the camera, but on an average day he could have been a stand-in for Jack Nicholson in *The Shining*. Sometimes he could just make a face and it scared me so bad that I'd begin screaming hysterically for my mother. And nothing delighted him more. He lay on the floor laughing so hard that he lost all control of himself. I inherited that laugh. Believe it or not, I miss those days. Perhaps I became addicted to my very own terror at an early age, which is why I chose a Stephen King novel over the works of Proust, Camus, or Dickens any day.

At any rate, give me a push is exactly what he did. My father always became a legend for his physical strength among those who knew him. He grabbed the back of the Big Wheel, and with all his might sent me hurtling straight down the hill on which we stood. The tree covered hill. How I avoided every tree on the hill is a mystery to me. I was going so fast that everything I passed was a blur, and the momentum made it impossible for me to steer. I did the only thing I could do—scream like a banshee and try to keep from pissing myself. Even over my screaming I could hear my father's roaring, insane laughter. I shot across the highway at the bottom of the hill and gradually came to a stop on the other side, by which time my mother and grandmother had both ran out onto the front porch to see what was happening. My mother began screaming at my father, who was doubled over from laughter, about how he was going to kill me. When they made their way down to me and my mother was certain that I was okay other than shaky legs and a heart that was beating like a humming bird, my father asked, "Want to do it again?" This time my head nodding was enthusiastic, and he began pushing me back up to the top of the hill in order to do it once more.

II

My memory really starts to come together once I started school. I can still remember every teacher I ever had, from kindergarten through high school

My mother and father moved to an apartment complex called Mayfair. We had an upstairs apartment in a long line of identical doors. When I went out to play, the only way I could find my way back home was to peek in every window until I saw familiar furnishings. My grandmother also moved into an apartment in the complex, one row behind us. This was the year I started kindergarten, and I remember it well.

Mayfair was in a rundown section of town, although not nearly as rundown as it later became. We were in the worst school district in the city, and on the first day I saw that I was one of only two white kids in the entire class. The other was my best friend Tommy, who also lived in Mayfair. Our teacher was a skinny black woman named Donaldson, and I'd be hard-pressed to find a more hateful adult. She wasn't as bad to the girls, but seemed to harbor an intense hatred for all male children. I honestly don't know how she ever became a teacher, as she seemed to spend all her time racking her brain to come up with new and innovative forms of punishment.

I was very quiet at this age, almost to the point of being invisible. I managed to avoid her wrath most of the time, but twice she noticed me. Once, for a reason I never understood, a girl told her that I had my eyes open during naptime. Every day after lunch we were to pull out our mats, lie on the floor, and sleep for half an hour while the teacher left us alone. No one knew where she went or why. For her it was not enough that we lie still, she wanted us to sleep, and expected us to do so on command. She appointed one person to be the class snitch while she was gone, and whoever she chose got to sit at the teacher's desk like a god, and look out over everyone else sprawled face down on the floor. The chosen person was always a girl—never a boy.

So, one day after lunch I was on the floor as usual, breathing dust and hoping for no spiders. The teacher came back half an hour later and asked the girl at her desk for the daily report—who had and had not been sleeping. The girl pointed straight at me and said, "His eyes were open."

I had not stirred from my mat or made a sound, yet this teacher made me stand before the class as she hit my hands with a ruler. It hurt my hands, true enough, and then there was the shame of having this done in front of the entire class, but the most frightening and traumatic part was the vengeance and hatred with which she carried it out. She was wild and furious, gritting her teeth and grunting with each smack of the accursed ruler. The one other time she noticed me I can't remember what, if anything, I had done wrong. I do remember the punishment though, and this time I was not alone. I had to once again stand before the entire class, this time along with two other boys, and hold a stack of books over my head for half an hour. All three of us stood with our arms straight up into the air and shaking with effort as we held a stack of books aloft. During the entire punishment she was howling at us in a rage, saying things like, "You're going to learn that I'm not playing a game with you!"

So much for kindergarten.

III

A couple of strange incidents occurred during this period of my life, both of which I remember vividly, but neither of which I can explain. The first happened while still living in the Mayfair apartments.

One evening as dusk approached my mother told me not to leave the walkway right in front of our apartment door. Being the unlearned heathen that I was, I beat it the moment she was out of sight. I ran around to the very back of the complex where a huge mound of sand was located, and proceeded to dig a hole with my bare hands. This was one of my favorite activities, in which I invested a huge amount of time as a child. I looked up from my digging some time later only to realize it was completely dark. I could see the streetlights on in the distance, and the night was deathly silent. No crickets chirping, people talking, or cars driving by. Nothing but the silence that comes once the movie is over and the screen goes blank. Knowing that I was now officially in trouble, I dusted myself off and started to make my way back to our apartment.

As I walked home I had to pass a place where two sections of the building came together to form a corner. The last time I had noticed this corner the apartment there was empty. Now it was dark, but the front door was open.

There was no trace of any light and the inside of the apartment was as void of illumination as some sort of vacuum. Standing in the doorway, propped against the frame with his arms folded across his chest was a man in black pants and no shirt. He had black, shoulder length hair and wore a shit-eating grin. His eyes followed my progress as I passed, until I stood right in front of him. "Where you goin', boy?" he asked in a way that said he was amused, but didn't really expect an answer. I said nothing, just stood looking up at him. "Your mamma's looking for you. You know you're going to get a whipping."

After a moment longer I continued on my way. When I encountered my mother, she had a switch in one hand and a cigarette in the other. I did indeed receive a whipping.

I never thought about this incident again, up until a day or so before I was arrested and put on trial for murder. I was eighteen years old, and the cops had been harassing me non-stop for weeks. My mother asked me one day after lunch,

"Why don't you take your shirt off and go in the back yard so I can take pictures? That way, if the cops beat you we'll have some before and after photos." Nodding my head, I made a trip to the bathroom where I took my shirt off. When I looked into the mirror over the sink, it hit me that I looked exactly like the man I'd seen all those years before in the dark apartment. Mirrors have always made me a little uneasy for some reason and this incident did nothing to change that.

The other bit of bizarre happenstance took place after we had moved from Mayfair and into a small trailer in the countryside. I slept in a tiny bedroom at the very end of the hallway. There were no windows, and only one way into or out of this bedroom. Fire exits? We don't need no stinkin' fire exits.

Late one night something woke me up. It wasn't a noise, as the entire place was deathly silent. I rolled over and found myself face to face with a strange woman who appeared to be fast asleep in my bed. I was paralyzed with fright. So scared that I couldn't move, couldn't scream, couldn't do anything. All I could do was stare at this sleeping woman, my eyes bulging in terror.

When the fear gave way to self-preservation I jumped from the bed and fled to my parents' room, wailing like a fire engine. My mother and father bolted straight out of bed to the sound of me screaming, "There's someone in my room!" My mother gave my father a scared look, but he was already on his way down the hall.

There was no woman found, and no way that anyone could have gotten past my parents' room to leave. There was no window to crawl out of and no back door to flee through. My parents pointed out these facts to me numerous times over the subsequent weeks, but I still couldn't sleep more than an hour at a time. I never slept the whole night through until after we moved, which we fortunately did very soon.

As I write this now I'm reminded that strange things happening in the night weren't all that uncommon in our house, no matter where we lived. In her teenage years I remember my sister waking us all up by screaming at the top of her lungs. Even a wordless shriek of terror would have been less jarring than what she screamed. Imagine being awakened in a dark house at two AM by bloodcurdling screams of, "There's snakes in the bed!" It happened to me more than once. She still insists they were there.

IV

Now I believe my mother and father just weren't meant to be together. Perhaps they weren't meant to be with anyone. My father has now been married and divorced about five times, and my mother follows closely behind in her number of failed relationships. The trouble between them began when I was in second grade.

My grandmother had gotten remarried the previous year to a respectable man named Ivan. He's the one I always remembered as being my grandfather on my mother's of the family. After the wedding my grandmother moved from her apartment to Ivan's house, which was in the nice, middle-class section of West Memphis. He was a nice man, in a nice house, in a nice neighborhood. There's not a hell of a lot more to say about him, other than that I grew to love him over time and cried like a baby when he died a few years later.

They hadn't been living together long when we moved in with them. By "we" I mean me, my mother, my father, and my sister. It was supposed to be a short-term arrangement while my father found us another place. We had been hopping from place to place recently, and in a period of months we moved to six different states before finally crashing to a halt with my grandparents.

My mother and father slept on the bed in the guest room while my sister and I slept on the floor next to them. I remember my father's strong arms picking me up off the floor on more than one occasion when he had been awakened by the sound of me gasping for breath, having an asthma attack. He'd carry me to the emergency room, which I despised because I knew a great many needles awaited my arrival. Now I actually look back on those days with a warm feeling in my heart, and I miss them. Times were simpler then.

We were there for a few months when my mother and father began to fight, though I still to this day do not know what they fought about. Perhaps it was the usual strain of being broke and on hard times. Whatever the reason, my father moved out and into a motel room.

They tried to work through it at first. My father came to pick us all up on weekends and take us out to eat, or to a drive-in movie to watch the latest horror release and fill up on hot dogs and popcorn. We always watched horror movies.

As a child I remember sitting up into the early hours of the morning watching horror movies with my father. Even now, on the eve of my thirtieth birthday and with a son of my own, I still watch horror movies and read horror novels because they remind me of "home." Nostalgia, you could say.

At any rate, it didn't work. I knew things between my parents weren't going to work out when I was walking home from a friend's house one day and saw my father's car in the driveway. As I approached I noted that the driver's side door was open and my father was sitting on the seat. One leg was on the ground, the other was in the car, and his face was hidden behind his hands as he cried so hard that his entire body was shaking. At first I thought he may have been laughing, until I looked up at my mother. She was standing outside the car next to him, with bloodshot eyes. When I got within reaching distance my father grabbed me and held me while he continued to cry. It scared the hell out of me, and I had no idea what to do.

My mother gave me a saccharine sweet explanation of how my father wasn't going to be living with us anymore, but that he'd still come by to see my sister and me on weekends. And he did for a while. He would come get us and take us to visit my aunt or grandparents on the his side of the family. It all came to a halt soon enough, though.

V

It wasn't long before my mother started seeing someone else. I was in third grade at the time. I felt a great deal of resentment towards her for this, and I clearly recall one day when she found me crying and she asked me what was wrong.

I told her that I wanted to live with my father, to which she coldly (and in hindsight, it seems, rather hatefully) responded, "Well, he doesn't want you to." I knew he had never said any such thing, but it still hurt to hear it. She was so ignorant that she couldn't imagine the depth to which such a remark wounded me. To add insult to injury, she informed me with a spiteful gleam in her eye that she had already told my father that she would soon be getting married, and I had better start getting used to the idea.

I don't want to paint my mother as being malicious, because I don't believe she is. She just was not capable of feeling things very deeply, or at lest not as deeply as I did, even back then. Not anger, love, hatred, or anything else. You could insult her, tell her you hated her, and she played off the drama of the moment, but the very next day she acted as if nothing ever happened.

At any rate, the moment she said that, I felt as if there was no comfort to be found anywhere in the world. I felt so cold inside, and there was nowhere to turn. By the look on her face, I could tell she took great pleasure in informing me of this. It wasn't a happy or gleeful expression—it seemed more defiant than anything. It created a rift in my heart. I felt like Jekyll and Hyde—part of me still wanted to seek some sort of comfort from her, for her to tell me that everything was going to be okay. The other part wanted to say things that would go straight to her heart and hurt her the way I was hurting. I wanted to spew bile and venom that would wipe the smug expression from her face forever. My child's mind didn't yet possess such magick words, though. It would be many years before I learned to spit hatred with that degree of precision.

So, who was this man that would soon become my stepfather? His name was Jack Echols and he was twenty years older than my mother, though you wouldn't guess it by looking at her. A steady diet of greasy fried food, cigarettes, no exercise, and a dead-end life had all come together to give my mother the look of years she didn't yet own.

After breaking up with my father she had started going to a protestant church not far from our house. I still don't know why, as I considered the activity to be pure torture. This is where she met Jack, who had been attending services there for an eternity, or at least since Jesus, the carpenter, built the place with his very own hands.

I can still close my eyes and see the first time I noticed him. Church had just come to an end, and I rushed out into the parking lot to play a quick game of tag with all the other little heathens (That's what my dad called me and all kids, by the way—heathens), when I looked up to see Jack walking out the front door with his arm around my mom. "What's this?" My mind snapped to attention like a dog's ears standing up at a strange sound. It only interested me for a moment, then I went back to what I was doing.

They never did go out on dates more than a handful of times, and it seemed that most of their conversations took place in that cursed parking lot. After church my grandmother would arrive to pick us up, being smart enough to avoid the place herself. My mother, sister, and I would all get in the car, then Jack would come dragging out at the end of the herd and cut a path straight to us. My mother would roll down her window and Jack would stand there talking to her until every other car had left the lot and our brains were cooking in our heads from the heat of the brutal summer sun. Years later when I heard the teachings on purgatory, that's what I imagined it to be like—not quite hell, but bad enough to make you curse the bastard hanging onto the window and forcing you to grow old in this desolate place.

Perhaps you will think me prejudiced in the manner that most children would be when they see a stranger/stepparent trying to take the place of another family member. I won't deny that such resentment existed, but I can also state that I've never encountered a single person in my life that had anything good to say about him. He was a hateful bastard who only grew worse with age.

When the courtship started, my mother was in her twenties, Jack was in his forties. He was bald on top, but he practiced the art of the comb-over. He had a ring of hair that grew around his ears, and he combed it over the top of his head, which was as bald as an egg. Most of his teeth were missing, and the few he had left were yellow and crooked like old tombstones. His skin had been cooked to the texture of leather by the sun, and his stomach was bloated with ulcers. I wondered what appealed to my mother about such a creature, but the answer is quite simple. Jack Echols was the very first man to pay attention to my mother after my father left, and that's all it took. She was striving for attention, and he gave it to her.

VI

Other than being distressed by the disintegration of my family, this was a fairly interesting period in my childhood. It was when I began to develop strong likes and dislikes, and to ask questions about the world at large.

I had recently encountered the concept of nuclear war, and I thought about it constantly. Actually, I dwelled on it in outright terror. I would look at the sky and think about how at this very moment a nuclear warhead could be speeding towards me. My entire second grade school year was spent awaiting the destruction of the world. I remember getting this idea from my mother, although I can't remember the entire context of the conversation. I do recall asking her how she knew with utmost certainty that the world would come to a fiery end through nuclear war, and she informed me that it was in the Bible.

This in turn caused me to look at the Bible as some sort of magick talisman that could be used for either good or evil, like a puritanical Magic 8-ball. I figured that if such information was in the Bible, then certainly all adults knew it. That lead me to wonder why anyone would launch these missiles if they knew it would bring about the end of the world. Surely they knew better, right? So who could be the responsible party? Only one answer made sense—it had to be the devil. The Bible said the devil was the bad guy, so he must be the one who would launch the nuclear attack. It made sense to me.

The only thing that could soothe and calm me during this era was music. That's continued to be true throughout my life, only my taste in music has changed. My favorites were Tina Turner, Bruce Springsteen, Prince, Stevie Wonder, Madonna, and Cyndi Lauper. My mother put my sister and me to bed and turned on the radio to sing us to sleep. I grew addicted, and still have trouble falling asleep without music now.

There was something very comforting about being in a dark, cold room with the music playing quietly. I didn't have to think about anything, the music took me away from myself, and I got lost in it. I needed it like a drug. It got so bad that I pretended to be sick at school just so I could come home and lie in bed listening to music. It was like being adrift on the ocean at night. Nothing else had the same effect.

My best friend during this period was the next-door neighbor, Adam. He was one of the most bizarre and unique individuals I've ever known, always into his own thing no matter what everyone else was doing. You couldn't take anything he said at face value, as he was the Baron von Munchausen of the elementary school. My grandmother listened with great interest as Adam told one outlandish and outrageous tale after another. He kept going for as long as you listened to him, and he was sort of like the traveling gleeman for our side of the street (we weren't allowed to cross it yet). His insane tales ended once someone gave us money for popsicles and sent us on our way. We both carried plastic swords and we enacted some of the more adventurous tales if we could find an audience who would sit still for it.

We spent every minute that we weren't in school together, and when his family moved away it left a huge hole in my life. I had no other friends because I had spent all my time with Adam. I became extremely lonely and didn't know what to do with my time. I spent my evenings watching cartoons and fighting with my sister.

Eventually I became friends with another kid on the street names Joe, and we stuck together even more than Adam and I had. Every weekend for years I stayed the night at his house watching MTV and eating fast food. Those were great times. Even after he moved to the other side of town, his family came and picked me up for the weekend. When my grandmother decided we were going on a camping trip, Joe came along with us. I don't believe we ever had a single fight. He didn't have the charisma of Adam, but he made up for it with his steadfast loyalty.

In our neighborhood the last months of the year were pure magick. From October through December I felt warm and content inside, never wanting it to end. I've spent my entire life trying to recapture that feeling, but have never succeeded. On Halloween the street witnessed roving packs of ghosts, witches, skeletons, devils, fairies, clowns, hobos and vampires. This was the heart of the southland, a Mayberry-like place the rest of the world has never understood. Everyone on the street knew each other and no one worried about poison in the candy. The adults stopped on the sidewalk to exchange greetings while we rang doorbells and yelled "Trick or Treat!" I miss it so much it can break my heart if I think about it too long.

Halloween was nothing compared to Christmas. I could say it was our tradition to put up the Christmas tree and decorations the day after Thanksgiving, but that was the entire town's tradition. Giant candy canes and Christmas wreaths were on every light pole, and banners saying "Merry Christmas" and giving the date of the annual Christmas parade were stretched across the streets.

At our house, my grandmother put her entire soul into decorating for the holidays. In addition to the tree (an artificial plastic tree that we pulled from the attic year after year), there were lights around the windows, wreaths on the doors, garland hanging from the ceiling, and a blow-up Santa Claus standing next to the television. There was even a small plastic tree standing on the kitchen table. Everything was incredibly warm and welcoming, and it felt like "home." I spent a great deal of time lying with my head beneath the Christmas tree, watching the lights flash. I listened to Christmas records my grandmother played on the stereo. Those days are gone forever, as is my grandmother. I can no longer even separate the memory of my grandmother from that feeling of home, and I mourn the loss of both every year. Nothing was the same after my mother remarried.

VI

My mother's wedding to Jack was nice enough as far as white trash shindigs go. I am very proud of my southern heritage, and our family has a long, strong southern history; more than one of our relatives fought for the Confederacy during the Civil War. I greatly resent anyone who believes the south contains only white trash and rednecks, because I consider myself to be the product of a long line of southern gentlemen. Anyone who doubts it need only look upon the imposing figure of my paternal grandfather to view the epitome of the specimen. He was dignified and reserved, well mannered, and carried the air of aristocracy found in gentlemen of superior breeding in the Old South. Jack Echols was no southern gentleman.

The wedding ceremony was in an old church that stood next to the highway. Our family came, Jack's family came, and any observer could point out who belonged on each side. Jack had six kids, the oldest of which was only a year or two younger than my mother. There was no music, no flowers, and not much of a reception afterwards. My mother wore a blue gauzy dress and Jack was in his shirtsleeves. He didn't even put on a tie. The ceremony was incredibly short, and after Jack slipped the minister ten dollars for his trouble, everyone climbed back into their cars and drove back to my grandmother's house.

There was cake and ice cream as if we were at a birthday party in hell. A photo of my mother cutting the cake was snapped, while I stood behind her grimacing. A friend saw that picture years later and said, "You looked just like Sid Vicious." I probably felt like Sid Vicious at that point.

After the cake was gone, my sister went to spend the night with one of her friends while I went with my mother and Jack back to his apartment—an ancient and rundown building that once served as a motel. The place was hideous and decrepit with green linoleum floors and doors that still locked with a skeleton key. It only had two bedrooms (really one and a half) and since three of Jack's kids still lived there, that meant seven of us would be cramped into this tiny space. I desperately wanted to go back to my grandmother's house.

I loved the school I had been going to for the past three years, which was called Maddox. It was less than a block from my grandmother's house, and I walked the distance every day with my sister and Adam or Joe. This school was another of those things that felt like home to me, but now I had to leave it behind for a new school, which I detested. I was stuck in this rat-hole apartment and this horrendous school (where it seemed that all the kids had overly large heads) for almost two years before finally moving back to a better neighborhood in West Memphis. It wasn't in the Maddox school district, but it was the next closest thing. The school was called Bragg Elementary, and its official symbol was a smiling bumblebee, which everyone proudly wore on his or her shirt.

The place we moved to almost defies description, because it was neither house nor apartment. It was the back few rooms of a church. A few months earlier Jack had forced us to start attending services at a place called "The Church of God." It was a real freakshow where people spoke in tongues and rolled around on the floor screaming when they had the spirit. The minister was a morbidly obese man who you could hear breathing from across the room.

Twice every Sunday, once in the morning and once at night, he preached about how the end of the world was at hand. Before leaving he always got out a bottle of olive oil and asked if anyone had any infirmities they needed to be healed of. Anyone who stepped forward would have olive oil smeared on their face before the minister shoved him to the ground amidst a flurry of shouting while a horde of rabid believers waved their hands in the air and howled at the ceiling.

This made quite an impression on my young, fourth-grade mind, and I gave quite a bit of thought to all the miracles I could perform if only I had that bottle of magick oil. My sister went up to be healed many times, because she had been very hard of hearing since she was a baby and always had to have some sort of tubes inserted into her ears. She never fell on the floor quivering, and never could hear any better.

Jack was pretty bad at this point, but not nearly so bad as he later became. He forced us to go to this church three times a week, giving us no choice in the matter. He was one of the most hateful people I've ever encountered, yet he was always in church. Now I know this is nothing unusual, that it's more the rule than the exception, but back then I couldn't comprehend it. He stood guard every night as he made my sister and I kneel down next to the bed and pray. We had a small dog, a Chihuahua named Pepper, and I once saw him punch the dog with a closed fist because she dared to hop up on the bed while he was praying.

So after going to this ghoul's wasteland of a church for several months, Jack announced that we were moving into the church itself. The back rooms of the church had been converted into bedroom, bathroom, kitchen, and living room, so that it could be rented out to bring in more money for the church. It wasn't bad, really. Only the kitchen and bathroom had windows, so the rest of the place was dark and cool like a cave. At least we had more room than in the apartment, and I was in a new school closer to where I considered home to be.

Jack only ever committed two acts of undisguised violence against me, and both were around this point in time. The first happened in the kitchen one Saturday morning. I was sitting at the table looking over my sticker collection, which I had recently become a fanatic about. I coveted stickers more than anything else on earth, and had quite the little album of them. My mother was cooking, and Jack stood blocking the doorway. I got up and tried to squeeze past him, with the intention of going to watch Saturday morning cartoons. I could feel the rage in him as he shoved me across the kitchen and into the refrigerator door, where the handle gouged my back. I lost my balance and fell to the floor. When I started to cry, my mother looked up with no real sense of urgency and asked Jack, "Why did you do that?"

He bellowed in a hateful voice, "He has to learn he can't bully his way around here!"

I had no idea what he was talking about, which only served to scare me. It's frightening to be punished when you've no idea what you've done wrong.

The second act of violence was a "spanking." I can't remember what it concerned, but I was arguing and pleading with my mother, attempting to get her to change her mind about something she had forbidden me to do or have. I can no longer remember what it was, but I remember Jack's reaction like it was yesterday. He grabbed me and slammed me down on the bed with such force that I bounced off and landed on the floor. He slung me back onto the bed and began hitting me with rage. The most frightening part was the way he went into a frenzy, cursing (this was the only time I ever heard him curse), and turning blood red.

What did my mother do? Nothing. As long as he continued to feed her the attention she desperately craved, she didn't care what atrocities he performed. Before, I had merely disliked him. Now the seed of hatred bloomed.

I said these were the only undisguised acts of violence, because he did so many other things—pinch me until I turned purple with bruises, bend my fingers backwards, jerk on my arms and twist my ankles—but all of these activities were just him "playing" with me. If he managed to make me cry, which was less and less often as time went by, his excuse was that he was trying to "toughen me up." The only thing that grew tough was my heart. Perhaps he was reminded of my father when he looked at me, and resented me for it. I never knew what caused his behavior, and now I no longer care. Over time I became crafty, and learned to avoid him altogether.

VIII

This is the same age (around ten or eleven) that I received my very first pet. Not a family pet—we had always owned cats and dogs, and even a bird or two—but my very own pet. It was a gerbil, and I had never seen one before. Another of Jack's quirks is that he couldn't resist stopping at every single garage sale he passed. One day we happened upon one where the family was trying to get rid of everything quickly because they were moving. They had a cage, food dish, water bottle, and some hamster toys—all for a couple of dollars. The catch was that you had to take the gerbil with it.

I stared, transfixed. It was amazing; this creature that looked like a large mouse but sat up and moved like a tiny kangaroo. I began to beg both my mother and Jack for it. My mother eyed the thing with a mixture of curiosity and disgust and finally gave in and bought it for me. They also began giving me an allowance of two dollars a week so that I could buy it food and whatever else it needed.

Before leaving the garage sale, the owner gave me a fish aquarium free of charge, just to get rid of as much stuff as she could before closing down for the day. I put the aquarium in my room next to the gerbil cage, and during the weeks when the gerbil didn't need anything I spent the money on fish. Soon enough the tank was full and I was obsessed with them. I did nothing but sit and watch them swim back and forth for hours at a time, and never grew bored with it. I was absolutely enchanted by them, and the gurgling sound of the air filter helped me sleep better at night.

My next acquisitions were lizards. I found a pet store that had them for ninety-nine cents, so I bought several and kept them in the sort of giant pickle jar you would find sitting on a bar. This was the beginning of a lifelong love of pets. From then on I was never without a pet of some sort, whether it be cat, dog, rat, bird, or fish.

IX

The gerbil, which I never even named, gained me a new name. In fifth grade we had a science class in which we learned about different groups of animals—mammals, birds, reptiles, amphibians, insects, etc. People brought things to class everyday to put on display if it had a connection to something we were learning. I decided to take the gerbil in as a fine example of the world of mammals. Everyone was amazed and impressed as they crowded around to get a good look. From that day on I was known as "The rat boy," not in a derogatory fashion, but simply as in "the-boy-who-has-a-rat-for-a-pet." The teacher's explanation that it wasn't actually a rat did nothing to change this.

My best friends were Brad and Clayton, and this is when I really started to get in trouble at school. It was as if Brad and Clayton brought me out of my shell. We all sat together at school and became an unholy trio of disruptive force. Our activities carried over into after school hours since Brad lived across the street and Clayton only lived a block away. Clayton was the only fifth grader in town who rode a motorcycle to school. We all three believed that the pinnacle of comedy was each other's misfortune. If you found yourself in an unpleasant situation you could expect nothing but laughter. A fine example of this was the time I found myself in a back brace and with several cracked ribs.

It started in a simple enough fashion, with the three of us hanging out in a park behind the public library. A rather overweight young woman happened to be enjoying herself on a swing, when her weight caused the dry-rotted canvas to give way and spill her onto the ground. She hit the hard-packed dirt and a puff of dust arose all around her.

We howled with gleeful laughter that only the very young or very evil are capable of. She jumped to her feet wailing like a banshee and disappeared down the street. We would have discussed the finer points of this comedic episode for days if not for what happened to me next.

I strolled over to have a closer look at the destroyed swing and realized the destruction was not complete. I could just manage to reattach the broken piece to the chain so that it looked stable. I turned and asked Brad, "Do you think it will hold me?" to which he shrugged his shoulders in a deceptively nonchalant fashion. Hopping into the swing, I began to kick back and forth, gradually getting higher and higher. My companions began to lose interest, let down because no pain and suffering were forthcoming. Suddenly at the apex of my ascent, the swing once again gave way and launched me high into the air. It happened so quickly that there was no chance of getting my feet under me. I landed flat on my back and all the air exploded from my body in one foul-tasting "whoosh."

Almost instantly the agony set in. I couldn't even scream, because I couldn't inhale. I couldn't draw the slightest bit of air and my lungs were on fire. I knew beyond a doubt that the specter of death had arrived for me.

I struggled desperately to roll over, trying with all my might to force out the words "get help," but no sound would come from my mouth. Amidst my terror and agony, what sight did I behold? Brad and Clayton laughing so hard they were about to cause themselves internal injury. Brad was doubled over, clutching his stomach and laughing so hard he had strings of drool hanging from his mouth while his face turned blood red. Clayton's head was thrown back as he roared his approval to the sky in the form of a giant guffaw. I could do nothing but cast them both the evil eye while thinking, *you sons of bitches*.

Gradually my ability to breathe returned, but the pain did not diminish. I managed to limp home, where I was taken to see a doctor. There wasn't much he could do other than put me in a back brace and tell me to refrain from shenanigans and antics for the time being. Jack Echols, in his infinite wisdom, accused me of faking it, although he could never come up with a logical reason why. It wasn't like I got to miss school because of it.

Perhaps you're wondering how I came to have Jack Echols last name. I allowed him to legally adopt me so that my father wouldn't be punished for being unable to pay child support. If my sister and I were adopted, then he would be free of this monetary obligation. My mother was gung ho about it because she wanted us to be seen as one big happy family, and to erase any and all traces of my father. She even made us call Jack "Dad." When I protested that I did not wish to give him such a title, my mother went into a veritable rage. She ranted, saying she would not have one of us calling him "Dad" (my sister) and one of us calling him "Jack" (me). I finally gave in and did as she demanded because the stress and the pressure wore me down. It's a form of torture to have to sit at the dinner table while no one speaks while an aura of anger hangs over everything like cloud. They wouldn't even look at me. It's impossible to even eat in such circumstances, and a child can't bear such psychological pressures. I relented, though I felt a sense of betrayal towards my mother that I've never gotten over, and every time I had to say "Dad" it was ashes in my mouth.

My mother now denies that such an episode ever happened. She has a very convenient way of forgetting and rearranging the past to fit whatever view she presently wishes to promote, much like the history changers in George Orwell's 1984. She now knows very little about me, but makes up stories so she can seem closer to me than she truly is. It gains her more attention.

X

Ah, all good things must come to an end as did my time in the church and going to the school I liked. The end came about when Jack decided there was some slight, subtle, and no doubt archaic bit of doctrine of the church that he didn't agree with. Perhaps it was the lack of snake handling. One never knows. At any rate, he showed his disapproval by dragging us all to another church as a means of protest.

The second church was even smaller and shabbier than "The Church of God." In reality it was nothing more than an old Chinese restaurant with a wooden cross nailed to the front. Just set up some metal folding chairs and you're in business. It was horrendous. We went there against our will for two or three months while still living in the other church. Inevitably, the obese wheezy preacher knocked on the door one day and told Jack we were going to have to move. The reason he gave was that they were no longer going to allow anyone to live there, but were going to convert the rooms back into part of the church. This was a blatant lie, as another family moved in as soon as we were out.

Our next house was a doozy. It was beyond a shadow of a doubt the worst place I ever lived, and ushered me into the most miserable period of my life. Even being here on death row is better than that little slice of hell.

Jack obtained this prime piece of real estate for the price of thirty dollars a month, and even that was too much. This was a real honest-to-god tin roof shack. The entire house consisted of four rooms covered with an aluminum roof. There was no running water or electricity to speak of, no heat or air conditioner, and half of the front porch had caved in on itself. By looking at it you would believe that such structures were inhabited only in third world countries.

During the summer you felt that you were being cooked in your skin. The sun beating down on that metal roof made the place so hot that you would literally think you were going to lose your mind and go stark raving mad if you didn't find some kind of relief. At night you would lie in bed sweating and being eaten alive by the mosquitoes. You had to wash yourself in a pan of water, so you never got truly clean. You would sweat even as you tried to wash. It's a good thing no one else was around, or they would have had to suffer through the stench of filthy, sweating bodies.

The winter wasn't much better, as the only source of heat was a small wood-burning stove, which filled the house with more smoke than heat. Your eyes always burned and your clothes always smelled of soot. As a youngster, my feet got so cold on many occasions that I wanted to cry. No one could stay awake all night to constantly feed wood into the stove, so it was guaranteed to go out right when the temperature reached its coldest point. When you got up in the morning, the temperature in the house was only slightly higher than the freezing air outside.

Looking back, the worst part wasn't the poverty, the heat, the cold, or even the humiliation of living in such circumstances; it was the absolute and utter loneliness. For many years in that old house, I didn't have a friend in the world to keep me company. It was far out in the middle of nowhere, surrounded by nothing but fields. No kids or neighbors to even speak to you. I was so lonely that I think even death was preferable. If not for my small battery powered radio, perhaps I would have died inside. Michael Jackson, Phil Collins, and the Fine Young Cannibals saved my life. If not for Huey Lewis and the News, existence would truly have been too bleak to continue.

Years later I read a book by Nick Cave called *And the Ass Saw the Angel.* It struck me because of how closely he comes to catching the feel of life out there. None of the more well-known southern writers like Carson McCullers or Flannery O'Connor could do it. It's like they may have witnessed life, but never lived it. Nick Cave comes damn close, though. More so than anyone else.

Books helped me to survive out there, too. The only places close enough to make it on foot were the courthouse and the library. I had no interest in reading anything but horror at this age, so I read the few tattered paperbacks housed there numerous times. I read Stephen King novels more times that Billy Graham read his Bible. He kept me company on many a long and maddening summer day. I still believe Stephen King's literary talents are far too overlooked. Everyone's too busy reading the story to notice the writing. Even if you took out all the monsters and creepy things, he's still a damn good writer. What other horror novelist can you say that about?

Later I discovered the ultimate horror—the Inquisition. The first time I stumbled across this atrocity was in a book by some demented adult that was titled something like, *The Children's Book of Devils and Friends.* It was filled with tales (and woodcuts) of witches having orgies, standing in line to kiss the devil's ass, eating children, and cursing people so that they went into convulsions. The book didn't explain that all these things were nothing more than the fevered dreams and insane concoctions of religious zealots that the educated world now knows them to be. It put them forth as being true, much as if they were originally published under the Inquisition itself. Then there was the additional horror of people being tortured and burned at the stake simply because someone accused them of being witches. It explained how they were strangled, burned, cut, drowned, and severed limb from limb in an effort to make them confess to flying on broomsticks to attend secret meetings.

It's not possible to overstate the impact all this had on my young mind. I would lie in bed at night scared to move, while my imagination conjured up horrific images. I had already had scenes of hell and damnation drilled into my head by Jack and his wonderful church folk friends, and these new discoveries did nothing to ease my terror. If I would have known then that in just a few short years I would be subjected to the same kind of witch hunt, that I would have some of the same accusations made against me, and that the same merciless zealots would imprison me and sentence me to death, then my heart probably would have burst of fright right on the spot. Who would have thought you could see the future by reading a book about the past?

At any rate, I was miserable and under tremendous pressure, believing I would burn in hell for all eternity because I couldn't stop myself from thinking bad things about people, not to mention the fact that I was entering puberty, and knew with absolute certainty that my uncontrollable lust was earning me a one-way trip to the lake of fire. I had recently discovered masturbation and applied myself to the act with utmost diligence. I couldn't seem to stop myself, and afterwards I prayed to God, begging his forgiveness. I had no idea that it was normal to have such urges; no one had ever explained such things to me. There was a non-stop war inside me—I wanted to be "good," but couldn't quite seem to manage it. My sexual appetite was insatiable, and I thought most people were morons. Yeah, I was on my way to the devil's playground, alright. It all seems so ridiculous now, but back then it was the most deadly serious thing in the world.

Oddly enough, this same children's book was where I first encountered the man known as Aleister Crowley. Now I know it was all propaganda, but at that young age I was amazed that someone could be so brazenly hedonistic and sinful. I've read much about this man and his life's work over the years, and it's incredible how little people really understand of him. His words have been misconstrued, twisted, taken out of context, and misunderstood continuously. If you don't know the key with which to decipher him, then you'll never understand what you're reading. Others don't even want to understand, and would rather use his name or image to sway and scare the ignorant, just as the prosecutor did during my trial.

After many years of study and contemplation, I now believe the only hell that exists is having to live in that tin roof shack in the middle of nowhere.

XI

This new Chinese restaurant/church was a bit more civilized than the last one. At least there was no one rolling around on the floor or speaking in tongues. There was no magick oil or spontaneous healings. There was plenty of backbiting to make up for it, though. Never in my life had I encountered more people who found it impossible to mind their own business than I found in that church. Someone was constantly whispering about someone else and then smiling to his or her face. Their entire lives revolved around this melodrama. Surrounded by such behavior, it was easy to see the type of characters who would stone someone to death in the old days. If put to a vote, they would cheerfully resurrect the practice.

The minister was a tiny, old, white-haired man who cried almost the entire time he preached. His wife could have easily passed for his sister, as they were the exact same size and shape, and there was even a resemblance in their facial features. They were the only people in the entire church who seemed to have any sanity left, and I believe it was their efforts alone that held the congregation together. Every so often they showed up at our house with a few garbage bags full of clothes. Their grandson was slightly older than me, so when he outgrew his clothes they passed them on to my family, for me and my sister. These were the only guests we could receive that didn't make me feel humiliated by our living conditions. That old man strolled right in wearing a three-piece suit and seemed completely at home, sitting on the couch and sipping iced tea. He often told stories about how he grew up dirt poor, and I felt no shame in his presence. Ditto for his wife. She never frowned, always seemed to be enjoying herself, and attempted to practice the art of conversation with my mother.

I don't believe Jack ever arrived anyplace on time, but especially not at church. Our transportation was a ten-year-old pickup truck and the four of us would be crammed into it every Sunday morning to show up at least ten minutes late. It's aggravating enough to be packed into the cab of a truck with not enough room to move, but on top of that you had to inhale the overpowering scent of cheap aftershave, juicy fruit gum, perfume, hairspray, and the exhaust that came through the hole in the floorboard. By the time we arrived I always had a headache and was in no mood to sit through two hours of bible thumping. Going to protestant churches became the bane of my existence.

The usual routine consisted of thirty minutes of singing, followed by an hour to an hour-and-a-half of preaching, and then twenty more minutes of singing to close the show while people waved their hands in the air, stared at the ceiling as if they were witnessing heaven, and shed copious amounts of tears. Every so often there was a surprise, like having a television set up. The lights were turned off, and a movie about the end of the world played. After it was over and everyone had the shit scared thoroughly out of them, there was a mad rush to the "altar" (a picnic bench). Everyone crowded together, huddled on their knees, and prayed that Jesus would take them home so they wouldn't have to face the horrors of the end times.

Once, quite against my will, I was even in a Christmas play. All the kids played the part of toys hearing the story of Christmas for the first time. I was a toy motorcycle rider, and one of my stepbrothers had dressed me in all his biker finery for the occasion. I looked disturbingly like Rob Halford, the singer from the band Judas Priest. Very few people can pull off that stereotypical biker look, and I am not one of them.

There was a constant stream of new preachers that passed through after plying their trade for a short while, because the congregation would vote them out. One night someone would call for a vote, and that would be that. It was usually the result of the preacher siding (or being perceived to side) with one or another faction of the congregation. If one group felt that he was showing more sympathy to one backbiting clique than another, he'd soon be sent packing. We waved good-bye to many preachers as they drove off into the sunset with a moving van full of furniture.

Meanwhile, back on the home front, our financial situation continued its steadily downward spiral, and the tension continued to build. We started trying to grow our own food, and it was hot, backbreaking labor. We had no irrigation systems, or even a hose and running water, so we had to haul water by the bucketful to our garden. Everything was done manually. Some days you go up one row and down another with hoe in hand, busting up the dry, cracked ground. Other days required you to spend hours hunched over, pulling weeds from between plants with bare hands. That task was especially hazardous, as you had to constantly be on the lookout for poisonous snakes, bumblebees, and wasps. If you let the monotony of the task lull your mind into a stupor you'd often receive a nasty surprise. After all the hard work, only about half the food was edible. The bugs and animals would have gotten some of it, and other areas couldn't be saved from rot.

The only thing we didn't have to do ourselves was crop-dusting. Our house was in the middle of the field the plane flew back and forth over, and it gave us a healthy dose of poison every time it passed overhead. If you didn't run for cover when you heard him coming, you'd get dusted too. I have personally inhaled enough pesticides to put a small country out of action. My mom and Jack's advice? "Don't look up at the plane, and try not to breathe deeply until he gets a little ways passed." I developed allergies so bad that my mother had to start giving me injections at home. She wielded that syringe in an entirely unpleasant manner.

You had to be certain you had all the food out of the garden by the end of summer, or there was a chance the fire would destroy it. Every year after the final harvest, farmers rode through the fields surrounding our house and set them ablaze with instruments that looked like flamethrowers. This was so that all the burned and leftover vegetation fertilized the ground for the next year's crop. I don't know what prevented the house from burning, because the flames came to a halt only a few feet away. If the wind changed direction you would nearly suffocate on thick, black smoke.

The one time that the house did nearly burn to the ground was because the wood-burning stove started a fire in the ceiling. The fire department had to come and spray the place down. Unfortunately, the trucks arrived in time to put it out. As I watched, I desperately prayed that the entire shack would burn so I'd never have to see it again. It survived with little damage.

Jack was a roofer by trade, and he started taking small jobs on the side, repairing residential homes to bring in a little extra cash. I started going with him, learning the process. I was only about thirteen, so mostly what I did was clean up the area when he was finished, and he'd give me a few dollars.

Perhaps up until this point I've painted a completely unsympathetic portrait of Jack. He wasn't an absolute monster any more than anyone else is. He was just a man, both good and bad. I believe he cared about both my sister and I, in his own way. He could be generous, and stopped to help every single person whose car was broken down on the side of the road. He always gave hitchhikers a ride, and was more tolerant of any form of self-expression I chose than any other parent would have been. I was free to dress however I pleased and listen to whatever music I liked. He had no problem with things like me wearing earrings, and I heard him tell my mother more than once, "He's just trying to find himself."

My mother was also a more dynamic character than she may seem. She always made certain we had enough to eat (even though it was junk food), she always went to open house night at school to meet my teachers, and she made sure that we got Easter baskets with chocolate rabbits. She tried to take care of us when we were sick, although she had no idea what she was doing. Sometimes her idea of taking care was to sit next to the bed as I struggled with bronchitis, and keep watch while smoking generic cigarettes.

I'm now at a point in my life where I look back on both of them with mingled feeling of love, disgust, affection, resentment, and sometimes hatred. There's too much betrayal to ever be completely forgiven. I am not like my mother who may argue with you one day and go back to life as usual the next. My grudge is always there, and my moods are not flippant. The best I can do is say that their good deeds may have softened the blow of the bad ones.

XII

Next to come were the joys of junior high school. Many significant events and rites of passage took place during the time I inhabited the halls of this repugnant example of our educational system. I had my first taste of beer, I had my first look at pornography, I took up skateboarding, and I met Jason Baldwin.

The beer and pornography were compliments of my stepbrother, who was actually a pretty decent guy despite having a drinking problem. He gave me the first of only two experiences I've ever had behind the wheel of a vehicle. He drove an old pickup truck with a jacked-up rear end and super wide back tires. One day as I sat in the passenger seat, listening to Alice Cooper on the radio, my brother tossed out the empty beer can he'd been holding between his legs, looked at me with bleary eyes, and asked, "Wanna drive?"

I responded with the phrase every southerner uses on a regular basis—"Hell yeah."

He pulled over and exchanged places with me, then instructed me on how to drive the last couple of miles to his house. He was extremely laid back (out in the middle of nowhere there's not much to crash into), and told me repeatedly, "You can go faster." I used to look up to him, but haven't seen him in many years now.

By this time all of Jacks' kids had long since moved off on their own, but this particular stepbrother, along with his wife and infant daughter, were forced to move into the tin roof shack with us after their house and all they owned burned to the ground. While there he taught me many practical skills, such as how to shoot and take care of your gun and replace the engine in your car, all while maintaining a beer buzz. I never did develop a taste for the stuff, and have never been able to drink an entire bottle. He'd hand me his girlie magazines while belching, "Don't tell dad I showed you these." All in all he was a pretty fun guy to be around, even though his tact was sometimes questionable (once, years later, when witnessing a neighborhood girl flirting with me, he called out a cheerful, "You better get on that, boy!").

My first year of junior high I befriended a mildly retarded and majorly weird kid names Kevin. I was most likely the only friend this kid ever had, and you couldn't make him shut up. It was as if he'd been saving up conversations his whole life. He could talk about literally anything for hours at a time—a cartoon he'd watched the previous afternoon, a magazine he'd looked at in the grocery store, or a new stuffed animal he'd acquired. This kid was a freak when it came to stuffed animals, and he had a huge collection—it's where every cent of his money went. I never had to say much of anything; he'd carry the entire conversation. He couldn't even make himself stop talking during class. Everyone else did their best to avoid him, so we had our own table everyday at lunch.

I believe the reason I didn't extend myself or try to make other friends is because I couldn't compete. We were dirt poor, so I didn't have the latest sneakers, I had no idea what videos were playing on MTV, I hadn't seen the latest movies, and didn't own a single article of trendy clothing. I didn't have to compete with Kevin. I could be wearing a sackcloth and have bare feet for all he cared, as long as I listened to him talk about his stuffed animal collection and nodded my head every now and then. Other than that, there were no expectations. I think pretty much everyone else in the world abused and made fun of him, but as long as I let him hang around, he didn't care. In hindsight, I also believe some part of me had given up. At the age of twelve or thirteen, I had already decided life was hopeless.

I had to repeat my first year of junior high, because I failed. I don't remember completing a single assignment during the entire year, and it showed when report cards were handed out—I had an "F" in every single subject. I didn't pass anything, and I didn't care. As the school year began to come to a close, I was looking at another long, brutal, lonely summer in what my family still refers to as "the white house." This year I carried an extra piece of darkness home with me. Right before we were released for vacation, another thirteen year old tried to commit suicide by hanging himself.

Joseph was a kid I had three or four classes with. He even sat right in front of me for one, and was never without a large duffel bag full of books, paper, colored pencils, protractors, and anything else you could possibly need to navigate your way through the seventh grade world. He was no friend of mine, but I knew who he was. A couple of weeks before the end of the year he stopped showing up at school. Soon the entire student body knew he'd hanged himself. He survived, but spent the next few months in a mental institution. The image haunted me all summer long with a power that nothing before had. I couldn't get it out of my head.

Late at night I'd lie in bed with my ear pressed to my little radio so that no one else could hear it. If Jack would have heard the slightest hint of music he would have thrown a fit and claimed that I had kept him awake all night. I wondered if perhaps Joseph had been listening to music when he decided life was no longer worth the effort. Did he wait until nightfall, or did he do it in the daylight? What did he tie the rope to? Did he jump off a chair? Why didn't he succeed? If I had said anything to him, would it have made a difference? It drove me to tears more than once. Lying in bed covered in sweat and staring at the darkness, I didn't even feel the mosquitoes biting me as I replayed the scenes I'd imagined over and over. I thought that if anyone knew how lonely and miserable I was, it was that kid. The anguish and the ghosts that haunted me evaporated like mist under the light of the morning sun, but would be waiting for me again when darkness fell. I couldn't seem to shake it off. That's how I spent my summer vacation.

The beginning of my second year of seventh grade didn't start out a great deal differently than the first. I wore my second hand clothes and collected my free lunch. Kevin wasn't even around this year, as it was decided over the summer that he was better suited to attend a special school for kids with learning disabilities. I was on my own.

One day a week during study hall we were allowed to spend thirty minutes in the school library. It was on one of these excursions that my life was drastically changed when I came across a superior literary publication dubbed "Thrasher." For those who don't know, this was *the* skateboarding magazine. This was the first time I had been exposed to the world of skateboarding. It wasn't just an activity, it was a culture. At this point I don't remember seeing any skaters in our school, so I don't know how the magazine found its way into those humble archives. That magazine became my Bible. All I could think of was skating, and after months of begging, I received my first skateboard for Christmas. It was a cheap, heavy thing, with no nose and very little tail. It was piss yellow, with a Chinese dragon graphic on the bottom. Definitely not the best of equipment, but it gave me my start.

Day and night I did nothing but practice tricks and read "Thrasher." I stared at the ads for the new decks like a sex fiend in the porn section. I also became acquainted with a different world of music I'd never heard of before, and discovered The Cure, Dinosaur Jr., Primus, Black Flag, Circle Jerks, and many other classics.

My grandmother moved into a trailer park with the dubious title of "Lakeshore Estates," and when I went to go see her, a couple of the neighbors gave me five dollars to mow their lawns. I saved the money to order clothes from skateboard companies, and began to replace the cheap parts on my board with better quality stuff, one piece at a time. Skateboarding became my life, and I did just enough work to get by in school that year. Soon enough, summer vacation was on me once again.

That summer was as hot, miserable, and lonely as the others, but it seemed to pass a little more quickly just because I now had a little life in me. I skated up the old deserted highway between the cotton fields, all the way to the courthouse and public library. Once there I made use of every curb in the parking lot until I was drenched in sweat and on the verge of heatstroke. If not for the old librarian allowing me to guzzle from her water fountain like a horse at a trough, I would have likely suffered terminal dehydration. I never walked anywhere—the skateboard became an extension of my body. I knew the name of every pro-skater, I knew who they were sponsored by, and I knew what tricks each of them had invented. I could have quoted any of these statistics to you without even having to think about it.

Skating had an unexpected side effect, too. It started when I noticed that people who saw me skating would stop and watch. I never thought about it before, but this made me realize I was actually good at something. It occurred to me for the first time that this was something not everyone else could do, and they were impressed with my ability. It gave me self-confidence and raised my self-esteem. I walked with my head higher and any inferior feelings withered away. It was as if I had become a completely new person. A new era had begun for me.

XIII

Going back to school the next year was vastly different because I was vastly different. I was no longer invisible. It seemed that a few others had learned the pleasures of skating, and we drew together to form our own little group. We had our own style of dressing, our own obscure references, and our own rules of conduct. The way we looked made it easy for us to identify other skaters in the crowd of students, and made it easier for them to identify us. Things have changed in the years since, but back then skaters drew quite a bit of attention, and often enough it was not of the positive sort.

Perhaps I stood out a little more than the others. One side of my head was shaved to the scalp while the other side had been allowed to grow long. I wore combat boots while everyone else had the latest Nikes. I had earrings in both ears and in one nipple. No one else even looks twice at that sort of thing these days, when even housewives have tattoos and every kid on the street has some part of their face pierced. A nose ring now is about as shocking as a glass of milk. Things were different in the South fifteen years ago.

My behavior wasn't exactly low-key, either. I was thrown out of class at least once a week for disturbing the peace in general. Part of the problem was that I was just so happy to be away from my hell of home. I mocked teachers, screamed out bizarre and nonsensical answers when they asked questions, and made a nuisance of myself in a plethora of ways designed to drive authority figures mad with rage. One teacher even threatened to "slap that bird nest off of your head" in reference to my haircut. I was delighted.

When I met Jason Baldwin, he was quite the opposite. I don't recall hearing him ever even speaking during his first year of junior high. I was the proverbial pervert who liked to amuse myself by looking up vulgar words in the dictionary during study hall. I certainly wasn't going to waste my time on such pointless exercises as homework. One day after exhausting my sexual vocabulary for the millionth time I slammed the dictionary shut and looked up with the intention of finding someone to bother.

Looking back at me was a skinny kid with a black eye and a long, blond mullet. He was wearing a Motley Crue T-shirt, and judging by the paper on his desk he'd been drawing and doodling to kill time. There was a backpack propped next to his feet which turned out not to contain a singe book. Instead it held a large collection of cassette tapes—Metallica, Anthrax, Iron Maiden, Slayer, and any other hair band a young hoodlum could desire. He often brought a small walkman with him, unclipped the speakers from the head piece and passed me one during study hall, or months later on the bus, so that we could both listen. I'd see him eating lunch every day in the cafeteria and nodded my head as a greeting when I was walking out. I never did ask how he got the black eye.

Jason usually had the latest "Metal Edge" or "Heavy Metal" magazine, and I looked at those while he examined my "Thrasher" collection. All of our interactions took place during school, because I still lived in the shack far outside city limits. The only class we had together was study hall, so there was little or no talking. Most of our communication was through gestures—finger pointing, eyebrow raising, head shaking, etc. This didn't change until one day when my grandmother nearly died.

My grandmother had already suffered one heart attack, so she knew the symptoms well. Luckily she had time to call 911, and then call my mom when the second one hit her. It was late in the evening when my mother began to shout that we had to go. We moved as quickly as we could, but the ambulance still got there before we did. We arrived in Lakeshore to see the paramedics bringing my grandmother out on a stretcher.

It seemed surreal because it was late enough that the sun was down, but it wasn't completely dark yet. The sky was a beautiful mix of dark blue and purple that made my heart ache. There was a special, magickal feel in the air that I've only felt a few times in my life. It touches something in you and it's so damn beautiful that you think you'll die because it's too much to take. A time like that isn't part of any season. It's not spring, summer, winter, or fall. It's a day that stands alone, like a world unto itself.

I've only experienced it five or six times in my entire life, but I pray to be blessed with more. It's like a drug. If everyday were like that, no one would grow old or die and war would not exist. There are no words that can convey the magick in those evenings. They're dark in essence, but look over you benevolently.

There was something about the way the red ambulance lights flashed through the entire world without making a sound that hurt my mind. No loud siren, just that red light flashing. I knew my grandmother would be okay. Everyone is okay on an evening like that.

My mother jumped from the truck and explained who she was. They let her into the ambulance to ride with my grandmother, who was barely conscious. We followed behind. At the hospital she was quickly rushed to surgery, where her heart doctor was already waiting.

We sat in the waiting room flipping through magazines without seeing what was on the pages, pacing the halls, and staring blankly at the television screen that perched high in the corner. When the doctor finally came out, after what seemed an eternity, he pulled my mother to the side and explained that he did what he could, but that my grandmother wasn't expected to live through the night. We slept in the waiting room, expecting to hear the worst every time a doctor passed through. The news didn't come that night, or the next day either.

That afternoon the doctor came to talk to my mother again. He said my grandmother was still alive, though in critical condition. The new problem was that she had developed blood clots in her leg, and it was going to have to be amputated. He had doubts about her making it through the surgery, but she would surely die without it.

We all lived in that hospital waiting room for nearly two weeks. I didn't mind, it was more comfortable than anything at home. The air was nice and cool, everything was spotlessly clean, and there was even cable television. Jack brought sandwiches from home to eat, or when he scraped up enough money, there were hamburgers from a fast food place. We only ate in the cafeteria once, because the food was so expensive, but I found it to be quite tasty. Every so often I snuck down to grab a few handfuls of crackers or breadsticks from the salad bar when no one was watching. I loved hospital food. I thought it was delicious.

When I was allowed to go in and see my grandmother she was so high on morphine that she didn't know what was going on around her. She weakly raised one hand to point at a mirror on the wall and asked me to change the channel. She called me a "little shit" and told a story about how we would become vampire hunters, because you could get a huge reward for bringing in a vampire egg. She only started coming back to reality once the doctor gradually decreased the morphine dosage. She was going to survive after all, though now she only had one leg.

A sixty-five-year-old amputee with two heart attacks under her belt, she was in no condition to take care of herself. She couldn't be expected to move into our filthy and squalor-ridden palace, so we had to move into her trailer in Lakeshore.

◆   ◆   ◆

I couldn't pack my few belongings quickly enough, knowing that this was my last time in the shack. It seemed too good to be true; I was escaping hell. I'd never have to see this place again. I didn't waste time taking a last look around, as there was nothing I wanted to say goodbye to. We didn't own a great deal that was worth taking other than our clothes and a few appliances. The furniture was all ready for the trash.

Ah, but I did find a treasure in that place before I left. It was a parting gift from the ghosts. There was only one closet in the house, and it hadn't been opened in years. It was packed full of clothes that no one wore and other assorted trash that should have been thrown out years ago. My mother and Jack decided to go through it to make certain they weren't leaving behind anything useful (yeah right, like a pirate might have crept in and buried a treasure). Jack was pulling things out and tossing them on the floor while my mother looked on. At one point he climbed into the closet so that he could reach an area that extended up to the ceiling. This was the area where the fire had once started. He handed everything he found down to my mother, and she tossed them out onto the floor with her nose wrinkled in disgust.

Suddenly something dusty and black was thrown out. Up until this point, I had no interest in anything they were doing. I was just eager to leave. Something about that dusty black bundle drew my attention, so I picked it up. It was a filthy, tattered, dry-rotted, and moth-eaten trench coat. My heart skipped a beat because of its perfection. I had to have it.

"Whose is this?" I asked.

My mom said, "No one's, it's just trash." I was slipping it on before she even finished speaking. "That's filthy, you need to wash it," she told me.

Jack, who had just climbed down, took one look and said, "It'll probably come apart if you try to wash it."

And that was how I came to own my very first trench coat. From then on, I was never without one. That seemed to be the one thing that people remembered about me more than anything else. Everyone who described me always began with "He wears a long, black coat." It became the symbol of all that people associated with being of me. That particular one eventually disintegrated, but I went on to find others. I felt safe when wrapped up in them, covered up and shielded. It was the greatest security blanket of all. I felt hidden when wearing it, as if bad things couldn't find me. Without it, I felt exposed and vulnerably open to the world. I was never self-conscious or a victim of self-doubt when draped in all that black cloth. There's no reason to fear anything when you float through the world like a dusty black ghost.

XIV

Once in my grandmother's "Lakeshore Estate," we had to build two ramps—one to get her into and out of the trailer, and one to bridge the slight drop between the kitchen and living room. It was next to impossible for her to navigate her wheel chair through the narrow hallway, so we put her bed in a corner of the living room. My mother and Jack took her old room, and at long last I had a room of my own. I rarely ventured outside that room while at home. It was small and dark, the light was encased within a smoky glass globe. I had a black vinyl couch to sleep on, and a small metal shelf to store my things. One entire wall was covered by a three-panel mirror. The closet had an odd folding door on it, and the floor was covered with short, brown carpet. I immediately covered the walls with pictures and posters of pro-skaters, and set up the cheap, second hand stereo that had been my Christmas present—I made it my place.

I've heard many jokes about poor people living in trailer parks, but I no longer considered myself poor. I was now in the lap of luxury—I could take a shower whenever I wanted, there was central heat for the winter, and a window unit air conditioner for the summer. The toilet flushed, there were no crop dusters, and we had neighbors. It was heaven.

This narrative would not be complete without a word about Lakeshore itself. People who have seen it in the many years I've been locked up have told me it's changed quite a bit, that it's no longer the same place. Now it's clean, the people plant flowers in their yards, and they wash their cars. People are neighborly and friendly, and even cops live there. Old people live there after they've retired. I suppose it is now be considered lower middle class. That's a big difference from the days when I knew it. To hear of these changes saddens me, because I feel that the last vestiges of what I knew as home are now gone. The world has moved on while I've been behind these walls. I no longer feel as if I have any roots. It seems that there's a whole new world out there, and I've become an old man in body and mind if not in years.

Lakeshore was a pretty big place, as far as trailer parks go. It consisted of about 200 trailers, give or take a few. They were nearly all run down and beat up, having put their best days long behind them. Nearly every one of them had a small yard surrounded by a metal chain link fence. The majority of those fences held dogs, which were the only form of "home security" we knew. Without a dog and a fence it was only a matter of time before everything in your yard was stolen and the gas was sucked right out of the tank of your car. The latter was accomplished with nothing more than a piece of hose and a bucket.

The heart of Lakeshore was indeed a lake. A lake so green and scummy that most fish no longer inhabited it, and you were strongly advised against swimming in it, because it wasn't wise to swallow any of the water. The bottom of the lake was an old boneyard of newspaper machines, wheelbarrows, box springs and mattresses, rusted bicycles, tangled fishing line, busted tackle boxes, broken fishing poles, and anything else your mind could conceive of. Before we went on trial the cops claimed they found a knife there. I don't doubt that at all, and I would not be completely surprised if they found a dozen more. My attorneys thought it was most likely planted there to make me look bad, which could very well be true. I also believe it's just as likely to have been dumped there by one of the many people who used the lake as their own personal garbage dumpster. That lake was a monster. I miss it terribly now. I now think of it as being beautiful in its own green, scummy way, although I can understand why those who lack my nostalgia would not. In my mind that lake has become like the Ganges, capable of washing away the pain, fear, suffering and misery caused by eleven years of incarceration for something I didn't even do. That lake has become a magickal thing to me now, and has come to represent "home" more than the Mississippi itself.

The streets around this trailer-lined lake bore the weight of a constant parade of stray dogs, shifty teenagers, and shady characters. It was what one might picture upon hearing the words "bad neighborhood." It wasn't safe to be caught alone, day or night. Roaming packs of hooligans tended to congregate around the small store at the entrance of Lakeshore, which contained two pool tables, and couple of video games, and a jukebox. You could purchase beer in cans or bottles, soft drinks (ditto), boxes of cereal, or the makings of a fine bologna sandwich. On the counter was a fishbowl filled with loose, stale cigarettes of every brand, all to be had for ten cents each. There were also several coin-operated washing machines and dryers, in which to do your laundry, but you had to have a sharp eye or else your unmentionables fell prey to theft. Jason and I spent a few idle hours there, along with his younger brother Matt and a few other neighborhood characters. After several years of seeing nothing but empty fields and crop dusters, this place seemed like a pretty happening spot. As long as you kept your eyes to yourself and didn't try to mind anyone else's business, you were fine. Anything else was asking for a fight. Some unknown marketing genius had given this establishment the quaint title of "The Lakeshore Stop and Shop," but I never heard a single soul refer to it as anything other than "the store."

XV

My first encounter with Jason outside of school occurred in the fall, sometime around the end of October. The reason I remember it is because in just a few days he'd show up at our door trick or treating.

I was sitting on my skateboard at the side of the street directly in front of the trailer. I had several pieces of wood that I was nailing together for about the tenth time to make a ramp. Most of it was old and cheap, more fit for the garbage than for construction. Every time I'd get it put together a bunch of knuckleheads came over to skate and the whole thing would collapse again. As I sat pondering the mystery of this endless cycle, Jason came peddling down the street on his bicycle. When we saw each other there was the instant spark of recognition. "You live here?" I asked, to which he responded that he lived on the next street. We just hung around for the rest of the afternoon, until I was finally called in for supper.

Jason kept coming over nearly every single day after school, where we'd sit in my room listening to music, talking, and laughing at other people until we reached a fevered, manic pitch. I laughed harder in those early days than I have ever since. It was the kind of laughter that causes you to lose all control and fall over. Years later Jason and I talked about those days, trying to remember exactly what had been so funny. Neither of us knew, we only recalled that it had been the most hilarious period of our lives.

Occasionally his younger brother Matt came over with him. Matthew at that age looked almost exactly like the Garth character from the movie *Wayne's World*. He was constantly trying to make a deal. You never found him without a piece of merchandise he was trying to sell or trade—cassettes, an old telescope, mechanical pencils, and all sorts of other things. The one thing he had in abundance was pornography. Matt was the porn king of Lakeshore. He waited until bums and homeless people had moved on, then examine the articles they had left behind. Nine times out of ten there were magazines. Bums may not have food, shelter, or money, but one thing they will always have is porn. Yeah, they had their priorities straight. Matt collected it, then sold and traded it to every kid in Lakeshore. I even had one or two of them myself. I remember Matt as being a businessman, one who couldn't sit still as long as there was a buck to be made or porn to peddle. He also wasn't above stealing anything that wasn't bolted down. Sometimes the capers he pulled off left Jason and I both howling with laughter, completely amazed.

At the age of twelve he walked into a grocery store, filled a shopping cart full of food and cigarettes, then pushed it right out the door, across two highways, and down the overpass back into Lakeshore. The memory of it still makes me laugh. At the age of thirteen he stood in a grocery store parking lot selling packs of cigarettes, the origins of which were dubious at best. Sometimes I think I miss Matt almost as much as I do Jason. It's hard to believe he's now grown, with a child of his own.

Soon every weekend found either me sleeping at Jason's house, or him sleeping at mine. When we were at my place we'd stay in my room trying to laugh quietly while eating chips, drinking cans of generic soda, and listening to heavy metal cassettes. We were trying to be quiet so that Jack wouldn't hear us—if he heard even the slightest sound he'd go into a rage, bellowing familiar phrases such as, "If you can't be any quieter than that, then you don't need to be having anyone here!" He went out of his way to make it unpleasant, and automatically hated anyone I befriended.

The very first night I stayed with Jason we decided to sneak out. I had never done this before, so I was doing it more for the thrill than to go anywhere in particular. The evening started out with Jason's mom dropping us off at the bowling alley in West Memphis, with the instruction to go nowhere else. As soon as she left the parking lot, Matt departed the scene in search of other excitement. Jason and I went inside to play pool and associate with all the other hoodlums. This was the hangout for degenerates and there were mullets everywhere we turned.

After playing a couple games and exchanging greetings with the locals we decided to go find Matt. Perhaps there were more interesting things to be found there. We crossed the parking lots of grocery stores and strip malls to reach Wal-Mart, which we knew to be his most likely location. While there we paid a visit to the music section, put our money together, and bought the newest Metallica tape, then sat down to read the lyrics. We finally found Matt playing video games, and we all three made our way back to the bowling alley, where their mom soon picked us up.

The night was so cold that every thing seemed crystal clear, magickal, and a little scary. The world suddenly felt very large. I remember every detail because this was the first time I had so wantonly and completely disobeyed all orders. We were free to do whatever we wanted, with no interference or adult supervision. A whole new world had opened up. The feeling of adventure and absolute freedom was amazing.

When their mother pulled up we quickly piled into the car and made our way back to Lakeshore. Back at Jason's place we all three went into his room to listen to the new Metallica tape and play video games on the Nintendo system and old television that sat on the dresser. I can't remember who first suggested sneaking out, but we immediately seized upon the idea. Time seemed to tick by at an agonizingly slow pace as we waited for Jason's mom and stepfather to go to bed. After the lights went out we gave them another hour just to be certain they were sleeping.

We made our exit through the window in Matt's room, because it was bigger than the one in Jason's room. We could also step out onto the fence by stretching our legs out as far as possible, and from the fence it was only a short hop to the ground. Jason and Matt had both done this before and had no difficulty. I, on the other hand, got hung up with one leg inside and one leg outside. They decided to "help" me by yanking on the leg that was outside, and nearly crushed my testicles in the process.

We had no particular destination in mind, so we walked the streets of Lakeshore for a while, leaving a trail of barking dogs in our wake. It was so cold that all the puddles next to the street had thin sheets of ice over them, and the streetlights sparkled on it like diamonds. I was giddy with excitement, and considered Jason to be wise in the ways of the world for having done this before.

We decided to pay a visit to the nearby train tracks, where Jason said there was a tree house in which some people sometimes left bottles of wine. To get there we had to cross an empty field, and we didn't take into account the recent rains. Our feet punched through the thin glaze of ice, and the three of us were standing in ankle deep water. Sopping wet socks and shoes are not recommended winter attire. The shivering and teeth chattering barely dimmed our sense of excitement and we plodded on.

When we finally made it to the tracks, not only was the tree house smashed, but the whole rotten tree had fallen over. We continued on our way, following the tracks for about a mile, with the intention of making a full circle and ending up back at Jason's trailer. We were quite a distance from any lights or trailers, and the night was silent. We talked of ghost tales and horror movies, urban legends and things we'd seen in the Time Life's *Unexplained Mysteries* books. Soon every hair on our necks was standing straight up and we were jumping at our own imaginations. We walked in a single file line, Jason leading the way, Matt in the middle, and me bringing up the rear. Matt insisted on being in the middle so that nothing could sneak up on him. In quiet voices we discussed how some kid had claimed to see a dead man hopping back and forth across the train tracks on Halloween night. It was like we couldn't keep from feeding our own terror. Sometime later I saw the movie *Stand by Me* and was overcome with nostalgia because of how much I was reminded of us.

Back at the trailer, we peeled off our wet footwear and fell asleep in front of the T.V. while watching *Headbanger's Ball*. I'll never forget a single thing about that night as long as I live. It's part of what made me who I am. I've often wondered if Jason and Matt have thought about it much over the years.

As we grew older, the thrill of sneaking out lost much of its appeal because in such a small town there's nowhere to go and nothing to do. Everything is closed by ten o'clock and there's not much thrill in walking empty streets after the first time or two. Instead, we'd rent low budget, straight-to-video horror movies every weekend and sit up all night watching them and making wise cracks. That was the closest thing to a "satanic orgy" I ever witnessed. The police, much like the inquisition itself, had a very vivid imagination. I'm inclined to believe they may have seen a few too many of those cheap horror movies themselves.

Often at the end of these festivities, we'd collapse into the bed to sleep until noon the next day. We couldn't fall asleep without music, and choosing our lullaby tunes involved careful deliberation. More often than not we slumbered to the sounds of Slayer, Megadeath, or Ozzy Osbourne. I never slept better than with Iron Maiden or Testament playing in the background.

Over the years Jason and I became as close as brothers because we knew there was no one else to look out for us. We shared everything we had—food, clothes, money, whatever. If one of us had it, both of us had it. It was known without having to be said.

After we were unceremoniously released from school for the summer vacation, we spent the long days sitting on the ragged dock in Jason's backyard, fishing, feeding the ducks, or making foul comments and put downs to whatever neighborhood teenagers showed up to hang out. Blain and David, Adam, Kenny, Carl, or any of a myriad of others showed up if nothing was going on. Sometimes we played video games, stared blankly at the afternoon cartoons on television, picked at each other, or listened to one of the geniuses make prank calls. Other times we'd explore out of the way places in search of snakes. In our neighborhood snakes were as valuable as cash and could be traded for anything. The days were slow and lazy, hot and long, each the same as the last. This was the extent of our lives, and we thought nothing would ever change.

◆   ◆   ◆

My first meeting with Jesse Misskelley was completely unintentional. One day after school I knocked on Jason's door, and his mother answered. Before I even asked, Jason's mom said, "He's not here, he's at Jesse Misskelley's." She called him by his full name—Jesse Misskelley—and I later learned that's what everyone did; I have no idea why.

Leaving Jason's front porch, I began to head back towards home, because I had no idea where "Jesse Misskelley's" was. I'd heard the name before, and from the sounds of it he was supposed to be one of the Lakeshore badasses. About halfway down the street I heard Jason yell, and I looked to my left to see him standing in the open doorway of the trailer. It turns out that Jesse Misskelley only lived about four or five trailers down from Jason. I entered the gate and Jason led the way inside.

The trailer appeared clean and kept up, no roaches or mice to be seen, and everything was in its place. Sitting in a living room chair next to the door was Jesse Misskelley. He was wearing blue jeans, a T-shirt, and tennis shoes. His feet were propped up on the coffee table, and he had a bologna and cheese sandwich in one hand, and an orange flare gun twirling in the other. His hands had something black smeared on them all the way up to the forearms, as if he'd been working on a car. There was a mesh baseball cap perched atop his head, the emblem on the front was a confederate flag and a grinning skull—typical truck stop fare. From beneath the hat long, straight, brown hair hung down to his shoulders.

Before my eyes even had time to adjust to the inside, a female voice screeched with deafening fury. "Get out from in front of the TV!" This seemed to be directed at me, and it came from a skinny, dark-haired girl sitting in another chair. This bundle of feminine charm turned out to be Jesse's girlfriend Alicia, who was notorious in certain trailer park circles. Some guys had their girlfriend's name tattooed on their chest. Jesse had the word "bitch" tattooed on his, in reference to Alicia.

Jason and I took a seat on the couch. The girl fell back into a silent stupor. Jesse became more animated and began to be-bop around the living room. He took a glass figurine from a shelf and started making kissing noises. "This is my girlfriend," he announced, holding up the glass figure. It appeared to be a small black woman with breasts bared, perhaps a novelty saltshaker.

An older man came out of a back room, and I took him to be Jesse's dad. I was correct. He didn't so much sit in the chair that Jesse had vacated as he collapsed into it with a groan and a sigh. He looked tired and weary, as if every day of his life had been a long day. He eyed Jesse's sandwich and asked, "That ain't the last of that cheese is it?"

Jesse's response was "oops." When his dad informed him that he'd been saving it for lunch the next day, Jesse pulled the cheese from between the bread and flapped it in the air. "You can still have it," he said while holding the cheese aloft and casting a grin in our direction. The cheese was several bites short of being a whole piece.

His father paid him no attention. Instead he said Jesse needed to get ready to climb under the trailer and make sure all the tires were on and aired up. They were preparing to move it to another trailer park called "Highland."

Jason was suddenly very ready to leave. As we were going through the gate Jesse called out "Y'all come back later so you can help me." Jason said "okay" over his shoulder without slowing down. A little farther down the street he told me that's why he rarely went over there—because they always tried to put you to work while they did nothing. Needless to say, we did not go back later to help, and Jesse took no offense. He knew he'd try to get out of unpaid manual labor, too.

I never did see Jesse a great deal, but we became familiar enough with each other to talk when we met. We'd run into him at the bowling alley and spend an hour or two playing pool, or hang out for a little while at the Lakeshore store. Jesse was no great conversationalist, but his antics could be amusing, and the odd things he did say were usually worth a chuckle. It was very apparent to anyone of even average intelligence that you weren't dealing with the world's brightest guy. He was a great deal like a child. He was harmless.

It's no great wonder to me how the cops could make Jesse say the things they wanted him to say. If they treated him anything like they did me, then it's quite amazing that he didn't have a nervous breakdown. They used both physical and psychological torture to break me down. They kept me in a small room all day long, with nothing to eat or drink, and no restroom breaks. One minute they threatened to kill me, the next they behaved as if they were my best friends in the world, and that everything they were doing was for my own good. They shove you into walls, spit at you, and never let up for a moment. When one of them gets tired, another comes in to take his place. By the time I was allowed to go home I had a migraine headache, I had been through periods of dry heaving and vomiting, with severe psychological exhaustion. I survived because if you push me hard enough I become an asshole. My point is that we were just kids. Teenagers. And they tortured me. How could someone like Jesse Misskelley, with the intellect of a child, be expected to go through that and come out whole? It makes me sick and fills me with disgust to think about how the public trusts these people, that they're in charge of upholding the law yet they torture kids and the mentally handicapped. People in this country believe that's the exception. It's not. Anyone who has had in-depth dealings with them knows it's the rule. I've been asked many times if I'm angry with Jesse for accusing me. The answer is no, because it's not Jesse's fault. It's the fault of the weak and lazy civil servants who have been abusing the authority placed in their hands by people who trust them. I'm angry with police who would rather torture a retarded kid than look for a murderer. I'm angry with corrupt judges and prosecutors who ruined the lives of three innocent people in order to protect their jobs and further their own political ambitions. We were nothing but poor trailer trash to them, and they thought no one would even miss us. They thought they could take our lives and that the matter would end there, all swept under the rug. And it would have, if the world hadn't taken notice. No, I'm not angry at Jesse Misskelley.

I get ahead of myself now, as all that came later. I still had a couple of years of freedom left at that point, and it makes more sense if I tell it one step at a time.

XVI

When writing about your life, it's impossible to include every detail, or even the most uneventful life would require several volumes to record. You have to look back over your life and ask yourself, "What really mattered? What were the big moments that shaped me, and made me who I am?" For me, one of those big events was becoming a member of the Roman Catholic Church.

As far back as I can recall, I've always been extremely interested in religion, spirituality, and spiritualism. For me those words cover a very large range of topics. I include clairvoyance, ESP, apparitions and hauntings, Druids, reincarnation and rebirth, prophecy, and even attending mass or praying in those categories. Beginning in about the fourth grade I had started to read books on Nostradamus, Edgar Cayce, astral projection, and the healing properties of crystals and stones. If it was connected to spirituality in any way at all, then I was interested. I believe this may have somehow been in response to all the sermons about hate, fear, and the wrath of God that I'd been hearing. I needed something that balanced that, perhaps.

One day while looking through the stacks in the library I encountered a shiny new book on Catholicism written for teens. It was aimed at teaching young Catholics why they do what they do during mass, or the meaning behind each gesture. I was about fourteen or fifteen when I found this book, and had never been to a Catholic church in my life.

I took this book home and sat up late into the night reading it. I took it to school with me and read it when I had a spare moment. I was absolutely entranced, and fell in love with the Catholic Church. All of my life I'd been forced to go to Protestant churches against my will. Now I wanted desperately to be allowed to go to a Catholic church. I wanted to see the things I was reading about, I wanted to experience it first hand. Genuflecting, holy water, praying with a rosary, the Stations of the Cross, but especially receiving the Eucharist—I loved it all. This was Christianity the way I had never before seen it—with beauty, dignity, and utmost respect. The entire process from the moment you enter the door, genuflect, and bless yourself is about respect, and about a dignity of the spirit. It was beautiful.

At first I was afraid to tell Jack or my mother that I wanted to go to a Catholic church. There's still a large amount of prejudice in the South when it comes to Catholicism. The word "Catholic" is often said in the same tone of voice one uses when issuing an insult. I once heard someone comment that a St. Christopher medal was "satanic." These days the South is the land of the Baptist Church, and it can be a cruel place for anyone not of that persuasion.

I knew Jack was the one that would have to agree to it, and I knew I had to tell him in a language he'd understand. So, one day I informed him that I felt I had a "calling" from God, and that I needed to find the place I was supposed to be. In the type of churches he attended, to say one had a "calling" meant that you were directly hearing God's voice or feeling his presence, and that it was compelling you to do something. What they refer to as a "calling" could be looked at by the rest of the world as anything from intuition to a psychotic episode. Still, he understood, and if I felt God was telling me to do something, then Jack Echols would be the last to interfere. He may not have respected me, but he would respect what he perceived to be "God's will."

When he asked where I wanted to go I knew I couldn't just blurt out, "The Catholic Church," because he would have looked at that suspiciously. Instead, I told him I thought it best if I went to different places, and that I'd know the right one when I found it. He nodded his head, and that was the end of the conversation.

Sunday arrived to find my family following its usual routine of preparing for church. Everyone got dressed and ate breakfast, then crammed into the truck for the joyless ride. The only exception this week is that I was dropped off at an Episcopalian church, while they continued on their way. I went inside, sat down, and actually paid attention to what was going on instead of shuffling my feet, playing with paper, or looking around at other people. It was nice in its own way—very pleasant and mellow—but it just didn't have the same aristocratic beauty I'd encountered when reading about the Catholic Church. I left when it was over and never returned.

The next week the process was repeated, only this time I was dropped off at a Methodist church. I wasn't as fond of it as I was the Episcopalian church, but I admit it was light years ahead of the places Jack usually went. I spent most of the time anticipating the next week, so I don't really recall much of what anyone said. I was focused on the fact that the next week I would finally be where I wanted to be, the waiting would be over.

There's only one Catholic church in West Memphis, and it's called St. Michael's. It was a small place when compared to the huge cathedral-like buildings used by the local Baptist churches, but it was well taken care of and in pristine condition. There were stone benches to sit on outside, and a small statue of St. Francis. The lawn was raked and there was no debris or even a stray leaf to be found on the grounds. The word I kept coming back to over and over was dignity. The place had dignity, and it encouraged all who entered to have the same. The entire atmosphere announced that this was not a place in which you will find people rolling on the floor and screaming.

I was dropped off and went inside to take a seat. I followed the lead of people around me, and kneeled on a padded bench to say a little "Hi, I'm here" to whatever power in the universe was listening. The place was completely silent—no screaming children or men in cheap suits bellowing obnoxious greetings to one another. Everyone quietly took their seats and waited. It was not an uncomfortable silence, on the contrary—it was very relaxing and peaceful, I could sit engaged in my own contemplations without fear of being disturbed. I felt very welcome there.

The organ began playing softly and everyone stood as the procession of the priest and altar boys made their way down the central aisle and to the front of the church. I couldn't take my eyes off of the small parade—the robes, the candles, the book held aloft—I was witnessing pure magick. I enjoyed every moment, and savored the experience. After the opening ceremony the priest spoke for about thirty minutes in a calm, quiet voice about what he'd just read. There was no shouting, he didn't beat his fist on the podium, and there was not one single word about the end of the world being at hand. I regretted having to leave once it was over, and would rather have spent the day there examining the scenes on the stained glass windows, admiring the statues that stood in the corners, or even watching the flickering of the votive candles.

That evening when Jack asked how it was, I told him that I'd found my place. When he asked how I knew, I said because it felt like home. He didn't say another word, and dropped me off again next week.

This week I waited around afterwards, until everyone had trailed out into the parking lot. I approached the priest, who was a small, balding man with wire-framed glasses. I introduced myself and with no preamble asked, "How do I become a Catholic?" We sat and talked for a while, and he explained how I had to attend classes, as there was a lot to learn. He himself taught the classes every Monday night. After getting all the information I needed I walked outside where the truck was waiting to take me home.

I attended every single class, never missing one. The priest arranged for me to ride with another woman, who also attended the classes. There were less than ten of us in all. Week after week, we learned everything from the teachings of the church on different points of dogma to how to pray the rosary. I enjoyed the classes almost as much as mass itself.

You needed a sponsor—someone who was already Catholic and could help you with anything you needed to know. Being that I had no Catholic friends or relatives, the priest introduced me to an eighty-nine-year-old man named Ben who agreed to be my sponsor. He took me to and from Mass every Sunday, and never drove over thirty-five miles an hour. He wore the same plaid suit coat every week. He never had a bad thing to say about anyone or to anyone. After mass we'd sometimes go into the cafeteria for coffee and donuts, and he proudly introduced me to other members of the church.

When the day finally arrived that I was to receive the sacrament of baptism and first communion, he gave me two gifts. One was the rosary his wife had used up until the day she died. The other was a suit to wear for the occasion. I was very touched by both.

The only time my mother or Jack ever stepped inside the church was on the night of my baptism and first communion. They sat in the very back row looking uneasy and out of place throughout the ceremony. When it was over they stood and clapped along with everyone else. I was happy that they came, because I felt a sense of accomplishment and wanted someone to witness it.

Ben and I showed up early every week in order to pray the rosary before mass, and even Jason often went with us. I told him he wasn't supposed to stand in the communion line, but he went anyway. The priest never gave him the Eucharist, but he still managed to get a gulp of wine each time.

I didn't stop attending mass until my life went straight to hell a couple of years later. I've long since outgrown any belief in mainstream Christian theology, and I even have some degree of animosity towards Christianity in general because of what has been done to me by people declaring themselves Christian, but I still love the ritual and ceremony of the Catholic church. A little old priest comes here once a month, and I'll watch as he gives the sacraments to the Catholic inmates on death row. I comforts me just the watch it, and I often find myself remembering the pleasure I used to take in it. I always promise myself that one day I'll return to West Memphis, perhaps when I'm as old as Ben and no one remembers my name, and I'll go to mass at St. Michael's, just to remember what it was like.

XVII

Going back to school the next year was like starting from scratch. I was going to high school, while Jason stayed behind in Junior High. After spending three years there, I had developed a sense of security or stability, and now it was gone. Even though the high school was only about ten feet away from the junior high, crossing those ten feet brought me into a whole different world.

Marion high school draws ninety-five percent of its student body from middle and upper middle class neighborhoods. This was a place where kids drove brand new cars to school, wore Gucci clothing, and had enough jewelry to spark the envy of rap stars. This was a place where I definitely didn't fit in. Everyone who used to skateboard seemed to have given it up and moved on to other things, which meant that my circle of acquaintances had grown much smaller. In truth, I wasn't even skating all that much anymore. In my new environment my behavior became even more outrageous, and I was viewed as a freak.

A freak was a definite group of people, but it's sometimes hard to explain what caused a certain person to fall into the category. Freaks weren't really popular, but everyone knew who they were on sight. One boy had huge mutton chop sideburns, wore short pants, and had stuffed animal heads on his shoes. Another guy rarely took a bath and had a tendency to show up every now and then wearing a skirt. He wasn't gay, he just liked skirts. A girl named Tammy (who I had a crush on) was harder to define. She was gorgeous and a gymnast, but wore nose rings, thermal underwear under her shorts, and white socks with black sandals. We had an odd relationship because she insulted me and created a whole new genre of derogatory names to call me, but jumped down the throat of anyone else who even looked at me funny. She verbally assaulted more than one young man who thought it safe to besmirch me, only to catch me alone the next day and call me a particularly foul name she'd dreamed up the night before.

I began an intense and unlikely friendship with a guy named Brian that year. He sat next to me in a couple of classes and was always very quiet, but in an arrogant fashion. He dressed as if he had a business meeting to attend every day, had immaculately groomed blond hair, and wore tiny, round, gold-rimmed spectacles. When he finished whatever work had been assigned to us, he'd pull out a novel and quietly read until the end of class. When he acknowledged anyone's presence, it was with contempt. I couldn't resist bothering him. When I demanded to see the book he was reading, he refused, stating that it was a birthday gift and I looked like the sort who would damage it. When I declared that I wished to try on his spectacles he once again refused and said he had no desire to clean my greasy fingerprints from the lenses. He seemed to think me an ill-mannered barbarian. These exchanged continued on a daily basis while class went on around us. He once hissed at me furiously, "Why can you not whisper? Even when you're being quiet you're still screaming." This came after several warnings from the teacher. He had never been thrown out of a class in his life, and had no intention of this being his first.

One day I noticed he had a cassette sitting on top of his books. I leaned over to get a look at the title, and it was no one that I had ever heard of. "What's that?" I asked. Handing me the cover so I could read the lyrics, he said it was a Christian rock band, and that it was the only kind of music he listened to.

I was appalled and outraged that such a thing existed—how dare they defile the sanctity of rock 'n roll! He claimed to have quite the extensive collection, was active in many fundamentalist youth programs, and never missed church. He even had the nerve to invite me to come with him. My first instinct was to make a nasty gesture, but suddenly stopped. Why not? It could be very interesting.

The function we attended was some sort of youth gathering. The church had a gym, and that's where we went. There were teenagers playing basketball, ping-pong, and even a few board games. I took part in none of the above. Instead, Brian and I took a seat in metal folding chairs at the back, so that we could watch everyone else. While we were talking a group of about five girls approached us, obviously friends of his, judging by the way they greeted him.

Despite what I had been expecting, I soon found that I was enjoying myself. I struck up a friendship with one of the girls that lasted for a couple of years—we talked two or three times a week on the phone, for hours at a time. Contrary to what my past experience lead me to expect, no one preached, tried to convert me, or seemed to be even thinking about religion. We sat and talked while everyone went about their business all around us.

It also seemed to be quite the hot spot for teenage romance. Just like any other place in which young people tend to congregate, you often saw boys and girls looking at one another as if they were about ready to eat each other up. We went back to this place several times during the year and there was only one awkward moment the whole time.

My appearance had been changing gradually. I allowed my hair to grow long and tangled until it looked like the character Johnny Depp played in the movie *Edward Scissorhands*. I no longer dressed like a skater—in fact, I now never wore anything but black. Any time I replaced an article of clothing it was with something black. I never again wore any color until after I was arrested. The awkward moment came when I showed up one night dressed as usual—long black coat, black pants, black shirt, and shiny, knee-high black boots that looked like they'd been stolen from a dead Nazi. This was my everyday garb. I noticed Brian was talking to an older man who I later discovered to be the "youth pastor." When he came back and sat next to me, he said the youth pastor didn't like the way I was dressed, as it appeared "satanic." Brian suggested that I should at least take off the black duster, so I did as he requested. His eyes grew large as he urgently said, "Put it back on!" Evidently my shirt, which was emblazoned with the Iron Maiden slogan, "No prayer for the dying," was a church "don't." I hadn't even thought about it before that moment, but it drew a great deal of attention from everyone else. That moment became one of the nails hammered into the coffin that sealed my fate.

As I sat in the county jail waiting to go to trial I saw that youth minister on the television screen. He was practically rabid as he ranted about "pacts with the devil." He seemed psychotic. Simply the fact that I wore such a shirt to a church function was enough to convince a great many people that I had to be guilty.

My influence on Brian's life crept in gradually. His manner of dressing changed, his hair grew long and shaggy, and he no longer listened to Christian rock bands. He soon fell into the "freak" category. He wore silverware for jewelry and chain-smoked clove cigarettes. He was no longer above sneaking into his mom's cabinet for a drink or two every now and then. He took up skating, and became better than I had ever been.

He was better because he was fearless. It was as if the possibility that he could fall and hurt himself never even crossed his mind. Some part of me was always scared that I was going to fail when trying something new, so there was a slight hesitation or a sense of holding back. Brian never had that—he hadn't yet learned that pain waits for you around every corner—and it was apparent just by watching him.

Soon I was staying at his place on weekends, or he at mine. On spring days, we went to the convenience store down the street from his house to get chocolate milk, Popsicles, and cigarettes. Then we sat on the curb and watched people going in and out. It doesn't sound very fun, but it was relaxing to me. I called it "people watching."

For some reason—I can no longer remember why—I began keeping an odd sort of journal during this time period. It was a plain black notebook with no special characteristics, but in the years since it has become one of the most embarrassing and humiliating monuments to my existence. Everyone else is free to forget their period of teenage angst. I am not. That damnable notebook is always there to remind me. To be honest, I'm always amazed that I still get letters from people telling my how much they've enjoyed reading the parts that are known to the public, and asking for more. There is no accounting for taste. I'm appalled that I ever wrote such trash. One day while watching my favorite sit-com a character on the show remarks, "Ever since they decided poems don't have to rhyme, everyone thinks they're poets." How true. He may as well have been pointing at me.

Over time the notebook grew tattered and filled with all sorts of things—quotes, bits of information, lines from my favorite stories, and "poems" that I myself had written. I can only bring myself to call them that with tongue in cheek. When I hear or read someone quote from them now, I want to crawl under a chair and hide.

The topics covered were pretty narrow in scope, limited to typical teenage bullshit: depression, loneliness, heartache, angst, free floating anxiety, thoughts of suicide, etc. All the things that people tend to outgrow and leave behind somewhere in their early twenties. Even after I tired of it I was enticed to keep it up by the only factor that has motivated boys since the beginning of time—a girl. She kept the notebook, and I forgot all about it. I never even saw it again until a couple of years later.

Not only did I find myself on trial for something I was innocent of, but they saw fit to rub salt into my wounds by reading my most private thoughts and feelings before a packed courtroom, television cameras, and newspaper reporters. Somehow this was considered "evidence." A bad hairdo, a black wardrobe, teenage angst-ridden "poetry," and a taste for hair bands is enough to send you to prison. Death row, no less. You'd think they'd install safety nets within the justice system for when such bizarre things occur. Evidently I'm the only one who sees the need.

Brian was my sounding board for such "masterpieces," and after hearing them day in and day out, he even decided to try his hand at writing a few. I don't know what happened to them, but I'm certain the world is a better place for their loss. Unfortunately, my own bad taste has been immortalized.

XVIII

On the last day of school our principal organized a huge "play day" every year. In hindsight, he was a tremendously cool guy to have running a school. He rented small, portable basketball games like the ones found in sports bars and arcades, and they'd be set up outside the gym. Inside the gym were volleyball tournaments and basketball tournaments, while outside on the baseball diamond the World Series of Marion high school took place. There were drinks, ice cream, and candy for sale. It was a day on which to say goodbye to the school year and hello to summer vacation.

Perhaps because I was somewhat lacking in school spirit, I didn't participate in any of these activities. Instead I wandered from one place to another, looking for other amusements. I went into the gym thinking perhaps I would find Jason, but didn't see him anywhere. I decided to sit in the stands and hang out for a while, talking to a girl who lived down the street from us in Lakeshore. As we talked, three of her classmates came to sit with us. One of them told me that she had been in my gym class all year, and that I'd never even noticed her because I was so busy practicing disruptive antics. I got along particularly well with one girl (Laura) and we spent the rest of the day hidden in the crowd, talking. The Lakeshore girl acted as a sort of mediator, and Laura and I were "going together" by the end of the day.

"Going together" was the high school vernacular which meant that you were boyfriend and girlfriend. When it was time to leave we exchanged phone numbers, writing them on each other's hands. We talked that night and set up future meetings over the summer.

◆　　◆　　◆

That last night of school Brian stayed at my house and we ordered pizza to celebrate the beginning of summer vacation. We sat at the kitchen table eating and watching the occasional person walk down the darkened street outside. When I informed him that sometime during the course of the day I had somehow acquired a new girlfriend, his curiosity was piqued. When I told him her name, thinking he'd have no idea who I was talking about, he was incredulous and asked more than once, "Are you serious?"

His shock came from the fact that he saw this girl and her two sidekicks on an almost daily basis, because one of them lived on the street directly behind him. We decided to call her, and it so happened that both the other girls I'd met earlier in the day were there with her. The one that lived right behind Brian was named Ashley, and we all decided to meet at her house the next day.

That set the tone and daily routine of our entire summer. Every single day after Ashley's parents had left for work, Brian and I headed straight over to her house where we spent the day, and all five of us passed the hours watching music videos or swimming in her backyard pool. The third girl's name was Carrie, and before the summer was over Laura and I broke up, and Carrie and I paired off. Brian and Ashley were an item all summer. There was something magickal about that season and the small group the five of us formed. When the summer ended, so did we. They went back to their world and we to ours.

We didn't meet them often on the weekends, because that would have involved the hassle of dealing with parental figures. We kept in constant contact by the phone, but no in-the-flesh meetings. Instead, Brian and I spent the weekends ice skating, riding around the streets of Memphis with his older brother, or watching videos and talking. That was the summer of much talking.

I also got my first job, and it was one of the most horrendous experiences of my life. I woke up one morning and decided I was tired of being broke and penniless, it was time for me to join the workforce.

I started by putting in applications at all the usual places that hire teenagers—grocery stores, fast food joints, Wal-Mart, etc. No one was hiring. Then one day I remembered a small seafood restaurant next to the highway. I had never been inside the place before, and I was growing desperate because potential employers didn't seem to value the exceptional intellectual giant that was presenting himself to them. The seafood restaurant was my last option.

I stepped inside the place one afternoon, and it was so dark that it took my eyes a minute to adjust. The floors were bare concrete, the tables were small and covered with red-and-white checkered tablecloths made of plastic. The cash register stood a few feet away from me, and sitting on a barstool next to it was a small, grey-haired, humpbacked man. He seemed to be engrossed in paperwork of some sort. I approached him and asked if this fine establishment might be hiring. He looked at me for a moment in a way that would lead one to believe he was calculating shrewdly before asking, "Can you start tonight?" I responded in the affirmative, and was told to show up at five o'clock.

I returned home elated. I had a job and would soon be able to afford whatever I wanted. The future was wide open and my mind was filled with possibilities. Reality would soon smash my youthful idealism.

When I arrived at five I was told that I was the new busboy. My uniform was an apron that looked as if it may have once been white in previous years. I distinctly remember using my fingernail to scrape off pieces of eggshell that were cemented to the front of it. After putting it on I was shown to the kitchen, where I witnessed a vision from the very bowels of hell.

This restaurant was the only place on earth that I've seen which was more filthy than prison. You could have literally vomited on the floor and no one would have noticed it. They would have stepped over the puddle and kept right on walking. The place was family owned, and the family consisted of a father, mother, and three children. The hunchback who hired me was the father.

The mother was a 250 lb. lump who never made eye contact with anyone and never spoke a word. She was filthy from laboring day and night in this kitchen. The three children—two boys and a girl—were hellspawn. The youngest son, who was only about two years old, wore nothing but a pair of filth-caked underpants. The older son, who was about three or four, usually wore shorts but no shirt or shoes. The little girl couldn't have been older than five, and she wore a set of super-hero themed underwear and T-shirt everyday. All three had crud-smeared faces, runny noses, and tangled hair.

The kids had to be kept in the kitchen and out of sight of any customers at all times. They weren't even allowed to use the restroom. Instead, they used a five-gallon bucket with a toilet seat balanced precariously atop it. This meant there was a five-gallon bucket of shit and piss sitting right in the middle of the kitchen at any given time.

The kitchen itself looked much like a room from the house in *The Texas Chainsaw Massacre*. The walls were greasy and stained black from smoke, the counter tops looked like tiny garbage barges, and the entire place carried the aroma of rotting fish. As a matter of fact my first task was to clean about ten pounds of spoiled fish out of the sink, which I did while continuously swallowing my own vomit. More than once I walked in to find the mother giving one of the kids a bath in one side of the sink as fish fillets or crab legs soaked in the other half. The first night, I moved a large bag of cornmeal to witness a large rat nursing a little of hairless pink babies.

I had been working there about three weeks when several of the other workers showed up at my door. They said they had to round everyone up and get to work quickly because someone had called the health department and they were coming to inspect the place. We cleaned, scrubbed, and hauled garbage from 2:30 in the afternoon until after eleven o'clock that night and still seemed no closer to making the place presentable. At that point I knew I couldn't take this for another second. I stood before the hunchback with my clothes looking as if they had been plucked from a dumpster, and every inch of my body covered in sludge, filth, and crud that defied any attempt at description. I told him that I was going home and was not returning. I couldn't escape it in my nightmares, though. I dreamed about the place for longer than I worked there.

◆   ◆   ◆

Brain and I began to drift apart once we started school again, for many reasons. One of those reasons was that I had once again failed, and would be spending another year as a freshman. This resulted in my celebrating my seventeenth birthday in the ninth grade. Coincidentally, one of my childhood heroes had managed to do the same. His name was Andy, and he was the only guy in eighth grade with a five o'clock shadow. He paid no mind to trends or changing fashions; he always wore jeans with the knees ripped out and a battered green army jacket. He had shoulder length black hair and wore a long, dangling earring that looked like a crucifix. Andy was the most laid back guy in the school and either slept through every class or drew. Nobody messed with him, and he didn't mess with anyone. During the summer Brain and I had gotten rides from Andy's little sister, Dawn, who was our age. She loved both of us, and was great just because she was so normal. She didn't care about high school politics and didn't fit into any particular group. She also consumed more vodka than a teenage girl should be able to.

Brain advanced to tenth grade and grew closer to the freak crowd. I completely quit skating and became what people now call "goth," though I had never heard the word, and there were no Goths in our school. I did what I did because it was aesthetically pleasing to me. In addition to Slayer, Testament, and Metallica, my musical taste expanded to include things like Danzig, the Misfits, Souxsie and the Banshees, and Depeche Mode. All the old skateboarding posters disappeared from my room and were replaced with old prints I found in odd books. Most of them looked a great deal like images from Goya's etchings and sketches. I caught a couple of filthy, vindictive pigeons and allowed them to fly around the room as they pleased.

I spent much less time with Brian and found myself falling back into the old patterns Jason and I had established. Brian was becoming much more melancholy, and one day in the fall we found ourselves standing on Ashley's street. He was looking at her house, lost in thought, when he asked, "Do you miss it?" I knew exactly what he was talking about, but still asked what he meant. "The way things were that summer."

I said, "No" and realized it was true. Of all the people, times, places, and things in my life that make me nostalgic, that was not one of them. By that time I had other things on my mind. I was in my first real relationship.

XVIV

My sister could not sing to save her life, but that never stopped her from trying. The problem is that every song sounds the same as the last when it comes from her mouth. My mother said it was because she was hard of hearing and couldn't make out the music very well, but I have my doubts. I'm more inclined to believe it was simply a lack of talent, but no mother wants to tell her daughter she sounds like a bag of cats being beaten with a stick. She was allowed into the school choir only because the policy was to refuse no one who signed up.

The choir director thought it was a good idea to hold their first concert less than two weeks after the beginning of the school year. The "concert" was to be held in the school gymnasium at eight PM. My sister put on her best dress and my mother prepared to drive her there and watch the show. Normally I have no interest in extracurricular activities, especially if it's a bunch of thirteen-year-old girls caterwauling their way through "Amazing Grace," but that night something compelled me. At the very last minute I decided to go along.

When we pulled up into the parking lot, my mother, sister, and Jack all hustled inside to take their places. I stayed outside for a while longer, dragging my feet and exchanging words with people I recognized. There's something very odd about being on a school campus at night. It doesn't feel the way it usually does. It's an entirely different place, and there's a crackle of excitement in the air. I was feeling this more than thinking it as I finally made my way to the gym.

I could hear the piano playing and people singing as I approached the building. There was a greasy yellow light shining through the front windows that suddenly made me feel as though winter had arrived, even with the temperature close to eighty degrees. When I pulled the front door open and stepped into the foyer, the click of my boot heels on the hard tile only increased the winter feeling.

Ten feet in front of me were two large wooden doors that covered the entryway into the main part of the gym. There was a girl standing with her eye pressed to the crack between the doors, looking in. Her back was to me. When she heard me enter she let the door slip closed and turned to ask, "Would you like a program, sir?" She grinned at me like she knew something amusing I didn't. Not a smile, a grin.

63

I've thought about it since, and there's a difference. A person smiles when they're happy. A smile indicates warmth and friendliness. A grin is a whole different animal, though. A grin implies pleasure. A person who grins is usually someone who is being pleased, even if it's your misfortune that pleases them. My grandmother used to say that when I grinned you could see the devil dancing in my eyes. That's what I saw that night—the devil dancing. It wasn't a waltz, either. More like a mosh pit.

The girl had skin as white as my own, and shoulder-length hair that was just as black, with no help from dye (over the years many sources have erroneously stated that I dyed my hair black. This is indeed its natural color.). She was wearing a pair of slacks that were so tight many would call them vulgar, and a low-cut blouse one could only say matched the slacks. She had a handful of programs for the choir concert, but I refused the one she offered.

I never went in to see the choir that night. Instead I stayed out with this girl who reeked of sex. It crackled off of her like static electricity, and was present in every gesture—the way she stood too close and looked up at you, the way she hooked her arm through mine, or cocked her hip to the side as she talked. She didn't seem to be able to control it, much like a cat in heat. It wasn't me that brought this behavior out, it was any man. I spent the evening entertaining her, and the sound of her laughter brought someone to the door to cast us a warning glance twice.

Her name was Deanna, and she informed me that if I'd bothered to look back I would have seen her in at least three of my classes. I didn't understand how I had sat in the room with her for almost two weeks and never even registered her presence. I blame it on the fact that it always took me a while to distinguish individuals from a crowd back then. When I was in a new class at the beginning of each year it was always one big nameless, faceless blob for at least a month.

We had lunch together every day after that night. We sat alone at our own table at first, but gradually a small but loyal group of people formed around us—other couples, two younger guys who had started trying to dress like me, and a large gentleman by the name of Joey who claimed to be my "bodyguard."

In the evenings, I'd always go to Deanna's house. Her family was very pleasant, a proper and quiet southern family. They invited me into their home and allowed me to take part in their routine. Sometimes we'd watch movies, play games, or listen to music. Nothing harder than country music was allowed in the house, and watching MTV was an offense that would get Deanna and her sister grounded. They could be very strict and even intolerant at times. After all the bad stuff went down, I thought they were evil tyrants who wanted to force religion down the throats of their children while ruling them with an iron fist. I still believe that's an accurate picture in many ways, and I often heard Deanna make declarations of hatred against her mother, but all the years that have passed have given me a new perspective. I can see both sides of the coin now.

In the beginning they accepted me as family. I didn't realize the honor I was receiving, because I'd never known anything like it before. I'd never before interacted with a girlfriend's family. Every time there was a family gathering I was invited. It's been so long ago that most of the memories have faded away and only the feeling remains. I can only recall a few of the more powerful ones. I remember being at their Christmas party, where Deanna gave me a stuffed gorilla and a tin of Hershey's kisses. We sat next to the fireplace eating bits of chocolate while the rest of the family laughed, and celebrated all around us.

The one memory that comes most easily to mind is visiting her grandparents, who lived far into the country. They had a large dog kennel where they raised hunting dogs, and a guesthouse stood nearby. Deanna's father had wandered out into a large open area for target practice. I was standing at the top of a hill and looking down at Deanna, who stood by a dry creek bed motioning for me to come to her. The side of the hill was covered in what I took to be brush. I figured the quickest way to reach her was to go straight through it, and began running. Going downhill gave me a speed I wouldn't ordinarily have had, and I loped like a gazelle through the chest high grasses. It was a wonderful feeling, almost like flying. Deanna looked at me coming down the hill and covered her mouth with her hands. I knew something was wrong, so I stopped. The moment I did I felt myself pierced in at least a dozen places. What I had thought was only brush was actually a chest high briar patch, and I now found myself in the middle of it. There was no way to move without ripping myself to shreds. She laughed and laughed and I ripped my way through, one step of agony after another, leaving little droplets of blood behind me. I was bleeding from too many places to count as she and I trudged back to the house, she laughing and me groaning. Her mother seemed to find it hilarious too, and laughed delightedly the entire time she bandaged me up.

Deanna was secretly a pagan. What was called a witch in the old days—a Wiccan. I had never before heard the term. All that I knew of "witches" was what I had read in the old books which said they flew to meetings where they danced with the devil and cursed crops, or caused babies to be born with birth marks. I knew only the nonsense passed down by the church and The Inquisition. She kept a small green diary filled with all sorts of things—names of ancient, pre-

Christian goddesses, plants and what their medicinal purposes were, and prayers written in flowery verse.

I had no idea that this was an old religion that would soon undergo a population explosion in the United States. Now there are many books written on the subject every year, and it's even recognized by the United States armed forces as a valid religion. Times have changed. Back then I had no idea that such a thing existed. I was amazed and flabbergasted.

I began doing my own research into the realm, reading about it and even meeting a group of local teens who were followers of the religion. They were a good source of information, but I couldn't stand being around them. They were all extremely flaky and melodramatic. I felt embarrassed for them, as they didn't have the sense to realize how socially inept they were. Wicca is a beautiful religion in theory, but I distanced myself with anything to do with it because I couldn't take the people. Many of them are people in their thirties and still trying to live and behave like teenagers. It seems to draw a great many people who cannot or will not grow up, and I have no time for such things.

It did serve me as a springboard into other areas of knowledge, though. From there I went on to learn of Kabbalah, Hinduism, Buddhism, Meditation, yoga, Theosophy, Tantra, Taoism, the Rosicrucians, the Knights Templar, and the Hermetic practices of the Golden Dawn. I couldn't get enough and devoured it all. I found it infinitely fascinating for a great while, not knowing my curiosity and interest would one day be used against me.

The beginning of the end was when Deanna's parents found out we'd been having sex. We got away with it for a while, but a simple mistake gave us away.

The very first time, we planned it out. When she was dropped off at school I was there to meet her. We immediately left and walked back to my place. We took a back path, following railroad tracks that kept us out of view of passing cars but also tripled the distance we had to cover. It took an hour to get there, and when we arrived we went straight into my room where we stayed for the rest of the day. My mother and Jack both knew, but neither cared. Fittingly enough, the soundtrack that played in the background was Suicidal Tendencies singing "How will I laugh tomorrow when I can't even smile today?" This became our routine.

We'd been together for most of a year when the slip occurred. The problem was that we arrived back at school a few minutes later than normal, and her bus had already left. I had no idea, so I left her there and returned home. She had to walk home. Her mother asked her why she hadn't told someone in the front office, so she could have gotten a ride from them. Instead of giving the typical teenage response of I don't know," she said she had told someone, and they refused to help. Her mother promptly went to the school to complain, only to discover that her daughter had never been there that day. That's when the proverbial shit hit the fan.

After Deanna told her mother the entire story, she was forbidden to ever have anything else to do with me. She wasn't even to speak to me. They couldn't stop us during school hours, but they made it impossible for us to meet once she was at home. I tried, though. I tried everything I could think of, but they weren't stupid. They even informed school officials to call them if she was ever absent from school.

We tried to work it out for months, but her parents were relentless, and it was like beating our heads against a wall. Early one foggy, gray morning she came to me and said she couldn't do it anymore. She couldn't take the pressure her family was putting on her, so she was leaving me. This was the last thing I was expecting to hear, because all we had talked about were ways to make it work. We had never even discussed this as a possibility. I was in shock, and my mind was having trouble comprehending her words. When the pain came it was like being stabbed in the chest with a blade of ice. She didn't make a long speech, so there wasn't a great deal of talking. I said nothing. She severed everything as quickly as a razor. "I can't do this anymore."

I turned and wandered away like someone who's been in an accident. "Wander" is the perfect word for what I did, because I didn't really go anywhere. I just walked. Walked and walked and walked. It became a hobby for me. I was the Forrest Gump of Arkansas.

The nights were the worst. Every night I'd wake up racked with sobs because of the dreams. It was the same general dream, with slight variation: she came and said it was all a mistake, that she's back now and the hurt will all be gone. Each one seemed so real that waking up almost drove me to the point of madness.

In addition to having to deal with this, Jack had now quit his job and was always home. Not only did he never leave the house, he never left the couch. He festered with hatred and made everyone's life miserable. The only time he spoke was to spew venom at someone, and he and my mother fought constantly. She started to get sick with a new ailment on a weekly basis because the stress was wearing her down. Jack always managed to make us the most miserable when it was time for supper. He'd sit at the table with a hateful expression on his face, almost daring anyone to speak. I just tried to stay out of his way, but it wasn't possible. He went out of his way to make sure everyone else was as miserable as he was. It was hard to swallow a single bite, much less make it through and entire meal while he was present. My sister later claimed that he molested her during this period, but I didn't hear of that until later.

I stayed out as much as possible. I didn't really care where I was; I just drifted from place to place, hoping to dull the pain. I took up smoking because the nicotine helped me fall asleep at first. Later it kept me up.

My life seemed to have no point. I went on living because that's what my body was used to doing. I drifted from one day to the next, not really caring about anything. I began sleeping with someone else just because she was there. Her name was Domini, and we later had a child together.

◆   ◆   ◆

Domini was a transfer student from Illinois, where she had been living with her dad. She came to Arkansas around the middle of the school year and moved in with her mother. This is a pattern she had repeated every year since her parents' divorce.

I was sitting through some sort of civics class when she came in. Deanna was sitting behind me (we were still together), and two friends, Joey and Jamie, were sitting on my right. The teacher was a bad tempered Italian man who had just finished lecturing us on how we'd have time to finish our homework if we weren't out riding around and "partying" every night. I pointed an accusing finger at Joey and voiced a loud and agreeing, "That's right," only to have him do the same back at me.

Deanna laughed, and the bad tempered Italian said, "Look at Damien, pointing them out." He gave me a narrow eyed look to let me know his comment had been directed at my crew.

There was a knock on the door and the teacher stepped out into the hallway. The class erupted, as it always does when there's no disciplinarian in sight. When he came back in, Domini was with him. He introduced her as Alia, and told everyone she'd be part of the class from now on. Joey shivered as though he found her repulsive. I paid very little attention. She was a red haired girl with green eyes who looked strangely like Axel Rose in the "Welcome to the Jungle" video. She was dressed in jeans and a denim jacket. I turned back to Jamie and Joey and continued to discuss where we would go that night once Jamie picked us up, much like the Italian teacher had previously accused. I didn't give Domini another thought for several months.

I encountered her out of school for the first time about a month after Deanna and I had broken up, and I was on one of my Forrest Gump walk-a-thons. Jason was with me and we were walking through a store a couple of miles from Lakeshore. Domini was there with another girl. I never did understand why she used the name Alia at school and Domini at home. At school she seemed painfully shy, never talked, and kept to herself. At home she was a little more comfortable and extroverted. The four of us began talking and soon moved over to the nearby apartment complex, where both Domini and the other girl lived.

A guy who lived there seemed to have an open apartment policy, because his front door stood open to let the breeze in, and people seemed to come and go as they pleased. I figured him to be a friend of Domini's because she wandered in and started talking to him as if she had just left. Jason and I followed. I sat in a chair minding my own business and staring blankly at the television screen while other people talked, drank beer, teased each other, or stood at the door shouting to other people in the pool outside. I didn't care about any of it, this was not my place and I did not fit in. I could tell Jason was just as uncomfortable. The only people I spoke to were Domini and her friend, who introduced herself as Jennifer. I wasn't there long before getting up to leave. Domini tried to get us to stay, but we said Jason had to check in at home. She wanted us to come back later, and I said I would, even though I had no intention of doing so. As we were walking home Jason asked, "You're not really going back, are you?" My answer was "of course not." In the end I didn't have to, as she came to me.

That night I was alone in my room with the lights off. The radio was on and I was staring at the ceiling. I couldn't sleep much during the night anymore; that was when the hollow empty feeling was the worst. At night there's nothing to hold your mind to the earth, and you spend the entire time falling into an abyss. The only cure is the rising of the sun. I was following my usual routine of waiting for daylight when my mother opened the door and told me someone was here to see me.

When I entered the living room, Domini was looking back at me. She knew people who knew where I lived and took it upon herself to come calling. It was late, and she only stayed for about fifteen minutes, but before she left, I kissed her. I don't really know why, I guess I felt like it was expected of me. I was still in mourning and felt no desire for her. In hindsight I know I did it for the same reason I walked nonstop—because I didn't know what else to do, and I've always figured doing something was better than doing nothing.

There wasn't much of a courtship and no scenes of seduction. We started sleeping together two days later. It took my mind off of things and gave me something to do on autopilot. It was something to lose myself in, and we established a routine. Every day Jason and I hung around the apartments where she lived, or she would come to Lakeshore. It strikes me now that Jason and I did a great deal of "hanging around," and must have appeared to be pretty shady characters.

Perhaps Domini saved my life, just because I needed someone to be near me then. I didn't want to be alone where I had to think. We had some fun moments together, but when I ask myself if there was ever a burning love for her in my heart I must be honest and say "no." Domini is a good person, straightforward and loyal, and she doesn't play games. She keeps things simple and never makes life complicated the way so many people love to do. Maybe I praise her so it doesn't seem so harsh when I say I was never in love with her. She was and still is a friend of mine.

One other thing of interest happened at this time. I heard a piece of information that wasn't meant for my ears and committed the only act of violence I've ever been guilty of. Early one morning I stood talking to a couple that Deanna and I had been close to, Josh and Lisa. Lisa let slip that Deanna had performed sexual favors for another young man while still with me.

If my wounds had started to develop scabs, they had suddenly been ripped off. This was a whole 'nother story, to quote Matt. Lisa immediately knew she had made a mistake, and if I weren't so white she would have probably seen the blood drain from my face. I knew just where this young man would be, so I turned to go find him. I could feel fire in my blood and a gleam in my eye that let me know I was alive. I hadn't realized how much I'd been dying inside until I felt that flame of life. I had no plan and no idea what I was going to do; I just let the current carry me.

I approached him from behind and saw something I hadn't planned on—Deanna was standing with him. This was new. She must have realized I knew by the look on my face. I was hurt and as mad as hell, and perhaps I was broadcasting it on some primitive, animal level, because as I came down the hall many people stopped and turned to watch. I still don't think my course was unalterable, even at that point. What pushed me over the edge was when I saw her glance nervously at him and say, "He's behind you." I felt a world of betrayal come crashing down on me. She didn't say, "Damien is behind you"—she said, "He's behind you." Like it was something they may have been expecting. I knew the whole story when I heard those words.

"Hey!" I screamed at his back. The moment he turned around, I was on him. He was bigger than me, and I'd never been in a real fight in my life, but he wasn't expecting the pure, raw fury that came from being hurt the way I had been. It happened so fast that all he could do was try to ward me off. He was backing up, trying to escape what must have seemed like a cyclone when he tripped over his own feet and fell. I went down on top of him and about twenty people jumped to pull us apart. As they pulled me off I desperately tried to hang onto him, grabbing at him, and left scratch marks across his face.

There was a rumor started that I tried to pull his eye out, but it wasn't true. I was just trying to hang onto him. This rumor spread and grew with time, darkening my reputation. Or as they say in prison, "casting a shade on my character." I was suspended from school for three days over this incident.

I regretted it almost as soon as it was over. It wasn't the guy's fault, he was just a symptom. I've wanted to apologize to him ever since, but haven't seen him in many years. I truly am sorry though, and I wish I could take it back.

Ah, but talking about such things tends to depress me, and a man in my shoes can't afford to become depressed. And we are talking, you and I. Just like old friends. Who else would I be telling my life story to? Let us now skip ahead to when things became more cheerful, however briefly.

◆　　◆　　◆

I had one of the greatest teachers to ever lend his skill to the realm of academic learning. His name was Steve Baca, and he taught physical science. What made him so interesting and effective was that he didn't stick to a script or enforce note memorization. He made you think. Sometimes he handed us a video camera, assigned a certain scientific principle to us, and then we had to invent and conduct our own experiment, while videotaping the whole thing. Instead of grading us himself, the entire class watched the tapes and graded each other. He showed us movies like *The Manchurian Candidate* and introduced us to the music of Pink Floyd. Sometimes we'd take the day off and play a quick game of baseball. This is a guy that made you want to go to school. He could also tell a joke that appealed to the teenage mind, a task most adults aren't up to. He was open to any topic you cared to discuss, and he gave advice. You don't find many teachers like that.

It was in one of his classes that Deanna came back to me. Mr. Baca had sent us out to work on one project or another, and he assigned Deanna and I to the same team, along with three others. It's one of the times that has fixed itself crystal clear in my mind. We all went into the gym, and one guy was holding the video camera while another guy and girl interviewed the janitor. I was sitting on the stairs and looking out a back door that had been propped open. Summer was just arriving and the sunlight was so bright it dazzled the eyes. There was just the slightest breeze blowing in. Deanna came and sat next to me, and I was scared to move or say anything, lest she move like a frightened deer. My throat closed up so I could barely breathe, and I wanted to cry. This was the closest she'd been since she left me.

"Want to talk?" she asked.

"About what?" I managed to croak. I knew damned well what about. My heart beat like it was trying to escape my chest.

"Why did you do that?" she asked, referring to the fight that had taken place almost a month ago by this time. We'd not spoken since. I shrugged my shoulders, not knowing what to say. We talked about other things for a while—the guy, who was now her boyfriend, and Domini, who was now my girlfriend, and whether or not I still wanted to be with her.

If I'd known then what I know now, I'd have run for my life. I didn't know, though. "Yes," I said, almost hissing the word, hoping she could sense the force and lack of doubt behind it. She nodded her head as if she'd just made a decision, then left me sitting there without another word. What did this mean? Was she coming back to me?

I never even came close to sleep that night. I felt like I was on the cusp of something big. The next morning Jason stopped by and we walked to school together. My nerves were too jangled to be much of a conversationalist.

Deanna was standing there waiting on me when I arrived, and indicated that she wanted to talk to me alone. I told Jason I'd see him later, and followed her over into what used to be "our corner." She was crackling with happiness as she told me she had dumped the other young gentleman. She said that since she had been the one to mess things up, she wanted to fix them properly. In a very official tone she asked if I would take her back.

I should have run like I was on fire. I should have shaved my head and taken a vow of celibacy. I should have instructed this raven-haired package of pain to go bugger herself. I did none of the above. Instead I crushed her to me, buried my face in the top of her head, and inhaled deeply. Her face was against my chest and she was breathing my scent. When I asked her what she smelled, her response was "home."

She asked if I'd broken up with Domini, and I explained that I'd yet to see her, so I hadn't been able to. She folded her arms across her chest and looked at me through narrowed eyes, but there was no real anger or jealousy, because she knew there was no competition.

Did I seek out Domini that night and tell her that it was over? Indeed I did. All was right with the world and I cared about nothing else. Domini has earned the right to call me an asshole many times over. I could tell her heart was broken and I offered no comfort. I couldn't get away from her fast enough, because I was living in denial. I wanted to believe the split with Deanna had never happened and the tryst with Domini never taken place. Because I knew that a vase which has been broken, even after it's glued back together, is never the same.

XX

It was amazing how quickly the hurt stopped. Humpty Dumpty had indeed been put back together again and he was a grinning fool. I sat slouched far down in my desk, lolling lazily as if there wasn't a bone in my body. Deanna sat directly behind me, tracing the pattern of hair at the back of my neck and laughing low in her throat when I shivered. She leaned forward to whisper, "There's only three days of school left. I don't want to lose you again now that I've just got you back." This is something I'd been contemplating but could find no solution to. We still had no way to see each other outside of school hours. After a few moments she continued, "We can still do what we talked about."

She meant leaving, of course. We had discussed running away together as a last resort. I hadn't believed it would come to that, I was certain a solution would present itself, but time was quickly running out. "I'll be your Huckleberry," I said, and never have I spoken truer words.

"Bring your things with you on the last day and away we'll go." That answer sealed my fate.

We talked about it nonstop, yet had no specific plan. We had no destination or goal in mind. We were going on an adventure, and our excitement was palpable. We settled on the vague notion of "going west." Neither of us had any idea what the magnitude of our actions would be.

When the final day arrived, we came to school as usual. We left when it was over, simply drifted off into the crowd, which was delirious with the realization that school was over for another year. No one even noticed us. It was a daisy of a plan, and came off without a hitch.

We took an extra long route that I had never before explored. In addition to Deanna and myself, Jason walked with us. If you're roaming aimlessly, then why not begin with the magickal land of Lakeshore? It normally only took about fifteen minutes to walk from school to our places, but this day it took two and a half hours of constant walking. We trod through empty fields far from any road, where there was zero chance of anyone eyeballing us.

At first Jason and I carried on with our usual bantering while Deanna laughed uproariously at our antics. She was amazed, because Jason never spoke in school, yet here he was chatting like a magpie. He and I could play off each other's words all day, until eventually we ourselves were incapacitated with laughter. Not many people know it, but Jason is pretty hilarious. He has a nasty, caustic, venomous sense of humor. After the first hour we got pretty quiet, though.

It was the heat, which was right at 100 degrees. The sun beat down on us without mercy, baking our brains in our skulls. On a day when the television was warning others to stay indoors and out of the heat, we were maintaining a strenuous pace. Every step we took sent bone-dry clouds of dust into the air, and my mouth was so dry I could barely speak. There was nothing but flat, featureless fields in every direction. No trees, no buildings, and no shade. Not even a living blade of grass. The three of us were dressed in black, which didn't help matters any. At one point I thought I would collapse from heat stroke. I was positive that I couldn't force myself to keep going, yet I still did, one step after another. One foot, two foot, red foot, blue foot.

We finally arrived in Lakeshore and proceeded to an empty trailer. The door was unlocked so we went inside and collapsed on the floor to rest. Even that hot trailer was a relief after facing the blistering sun. I handed Jason a wad of sweat soaked dollar bills and moaned "drinks." He left and made his way to the Lakeshore store. While he was gone Deanna changed into a set of my clothes that weren't wet with sweat, as I'd had the presence of mind to bring along some extras. I didn't bother changing, but I became obsessed with one idea. All I could think about was how wonderful it would be to wait until nightfall, then slip into that cool, crusty green lake. I no longer cared that it was filthier than a septic tank; I could practically feel its coolness against my skin. My tongue was stuck to the roof of my mouth. We were alone, but so hot, tired, and nauseous that we could do nothing.

Jason finally returned with a paper sack of Mountain Dews and Dr. Peppers. I drained a Mountain Dew in one long swallow then popped open a Dr. Pepper to drink at a more sedated pace. I felt life returning to me. He'd even had the wisdom to pick up some candy bars, so I quickly scarfed one of those. Full of sugar and caffeine, I was ready to juke and jive.

I investigated my surroundings while Jason told me breathlessly, "Man, every freak in the world is out there." When I suggested it might help if he were slightly more articulate, he explained that all the neighborhood kids were looking for me like a pack of hounds, because the police had been through looking for me, and they were now convinced they might receive some sort of reward for finding me. It seemed Deanna's parents had wasted no time in calling the authorities to report her missing once they realized skullduggery was afoot.

"No shit?" I asked as I sat down in front of a piano, the only piece of furniture in the entire place. I found it slightly odd that someone lived in a trailer park but could still afford a piano. A few of the keys were busted, but I could still manage to play it a little, which I did while Jason told me they had tried to follow him, thinking he'd lead them to me. Deanna came and sat next to me on the piano bench while Jason peeked out a window. He turned to me and said something that hadn't crossed my mind—"You better stop that, because if one of those freaks hear a piano playing in here they're going to be pretty sure it's not a ghost." I snatched my fingers from the keys.

I sat quietly in thought for a few minutes before telling Jason that Deanna and I would sleep there that night, then say goodbye to him in the morning. There was no chance of him going with us because he was the only pillar of stability in his home. If he was not there to take care of his brothers then they would go feral like the Lakeshore dogs. He truly did have to be like a father figure to them, and I was always impressed by how competently he handled the task. Most people twice his age couldn't do the job half as well. He exited the scene to go make supper for them.

The moment he was gone Deanna and I fell upon one another. Within seconds we were engaged in the act of sexual congress. Next came a mystery that I have never found the key to. Somehow, we were found.

For the last half-hour the sky had grown steadily darker, until the sun that had scorched us earlier was no longer visible. It was not the approach of night, but signaled the coming of one big, god-almighty storm. The wind picked up until I was absolutely certain a tornado would arrive at any moment. Would it not be ironic if we escaped parental control only to meet our doom at the hand of Mother Nature's great destroyer of trailer parks, the mighty tornado? Such was not our fate. The sky grew black as night and the wind continued to howl and blow so fiercely that it seemed the trailer would roll over, but not a single drop of rain fell.

The wind suddenly stopped. It didn't die down, it just stopped all at once. A really bad feeling rippled up my spine. I stopped what I was doing and cocked my head to the side like a dog listening for a strange sound. "What is it?" Deanna asked.

I waited seconds before reluctantly admitting, "I don't know." All I knew was that my every cell had just been flooded with the fight-or-flight feeling, and I had a terrible sense of urgency.

"Then pay attention to me," she said.

Just as I leaned forward to kiss her I heard glass shatter. "Shit!" I hissed as we grabbed our clothes. Even though I knew it was pointless and the jig was up, we still attempted to hide. It was a cop. Instead of opening the door and walking in, he felt the need to smash in a window and fulfill some sort of swat team fantasy. He later lied and said that we had busted out the window.

He was a real piece of work—about four and a half feet tall, with the sort of mustache you only see on cops or gay '70s porn stars. He was the kind of guy that needed a badge and gun just to stop people from laughing at him. I'm certain he heard us moving because he came right to where we were and started jerking us around.

As he was escorting us out, Deanna's father approached. He put his hand on my shoulder and began breathing hard, as if he were having trouble restraining himself. I looked straight into his eyes and grinned like a jackal. I wanted him to be able to look into my soul and see how much pain he had already caused me. I wanted him to know he could do nothing to me that was worse than what I'd already been through. The cop pushed him away and said, "Relax, just let me handle it." He backed off and the cop put Deanna and me both in the back of his car before returning to talk to her mother and father. I noticed that even her older sister had come out for the occasion, and I gave her my most charming smile.

While we sat in the car she held my hands and said, "Whatever happens, you have to come find me." I promised that I would, no matter what. She kissed me then, like she had seen the future. It was the last time we would ever touch. Another cop had pulled up, and they split us up, putting her in his car. She blew a kiss at me and waved goodbye as it drove off.

◆   ◆   ◆

I arrived at the county jail and was escorted to my suite. It was a dark, dank cell that smelled of feet and corn chips, a tiny space with a brown solid steel door. There was no entertainment except the graffiti, which covered every square inch of the walls. I was amazed at the bits of information people had thought important enough to write there. For instance, someone thought it vital that the world know someone named "Pimp hen" was adept at certain sexual maneuvers. I felt a bit like an archeologist in a tomb.

I was left alone for what I estimated to be two or three hours, but it's impossible to really tell time in a place like that. It's a form of mental torture, and I only knew that it seemed like an eternity. I kept wondering, "Where is she? Is she in this building? Do they have her in a filthy rat hole like this one?" The graffiti offered no answers to these questions. I was pacing like an animal when a guard came and opened the door, motioning for me to follow. I was lead to an office in which sat a bloated, corpulent man with beady little rat's eyes. Jerry Driver and I had come face to face for the first time.

He seemed to have a pleasant enough attitude as he introduced himself. He started asking questions and I answered honestly, thinking there was no reason not to. He asked why we were in the trailer, and I told him we had run away because her parents wouldn't leave us alone. No, we didn't know where we were going, and no, we didn't know what we were going to do once we got there. We figured it would come to us in time.

This is where things started getting weird. The smile never left his face, which looked like folds of uncooked dough. "Have you heard anything about Satanists around town?"

I thought that a bit odd, but answered, "No."

He continued to press on—"You haven't heard anything about Satanists, plans to commit sacrifices or break into churches?" His beady little rat's eyes gleamed at me, like he was really starting to get off on thinking about this stuff. You could tell something just wasn't right about him.

I was pretty certain I would have remembered a roving pack of bloodthirsty devil worshipers if they had passed me on the street while chatting about such topics, so I told him, "I'm pretty certain I don't." He seemed to be considering something as he chewed his bottom lip with tiny, yellow stained, rat teeth. Finally he shifted his obese bulk to pull something out of his desk.

I could practically see his whiskers twitch as he said, "What can you tell me about this?" The object he held was Deanna's little green diary. I wanted to reach out for it, but knew it was pointless. I brushed aside his question, knowing that it would be like trying to explain something to the Spanish inquisition.

"Where is she?" It was my turn to ask questions. He told me she was being held at a women's detention center in a town called Helena. He watched me closely as he said she had had "psychiatric trouble" in the past, and her parents thought it might be best if she was sent for treatment. She was being held until tomorrow, when she would be transported to a psychiatric hospital in Memphis. This was news to me. I knew nothing of any past "psychiatric trouble." It may not have even been true, because I soon learned that you could believe nothing he said. I didn't know that then, and sat there seeing images of Deanna in an insane asylum. All I could picture was the Anthrax video called "Madhouse," in which everyone wore straight jackets.

I was told I'd spend the next week in Jonesboro where someone would come talk to me. Jerry Driver himself drove me there. It was a jail. Everyone wore an orange jumpsuit that said "Craighead County" on the back, and you slept in a cell. There was a day room where inmates played Uno with an ancient deck of greasy, creased cards. Time seemed to come to an absolute standstill. Later I discovered that it made no sense for me to be there, because anyone else who had been picked up the way we were would have received nothing more serious than a warning or a year of probation at the most, before being sent home. Deanna and I were being put in jail because Jerry Driver was not finished with us.

One day I was escorted to see a mountain of a woman who looked like she applied her make-up with a spatula. She talked to me for about an hour then gave me a test, which consisted of showing me flashcards before telling Jerry Driver, "we have a bed for him." I was puzzled about the meaning of this until it was explained that I myself would be going to a psychiatric hospital within the next few days. I suddenly saw myself in that "Madhouse" video.

◆   ◆   ◆

I was left in the jail while they made arrangements for me to take a vacation in the nuthouse. I had about three days to wait for my transportation, and during that time I continuously paced from one end of the cellblock to the other. There were about ten to fifteen other guys there at any given time, and I later learned they were all typical jailbirds. I say "typical" because over the years I've had the opportunity to observe many people behind bars, and most of them have a tremendous amount in common. I've always come to the same conclusion—it's no wonder these guys are where they are.

There's not much to do in jail, so one day I thought I'd call home and check up. My mother knew I was leaving home, and had even given me a little money. She went to court when Jerry Driver argued before a judge that he should be allowed to keep me in jail instead of allowing me to go home, as would normally be done. I called my mother to see if perhaps she knew more than I did. I was in for quite a shock. My father was back.

It seems that mother finally came to her senses and gave Jack the boot. It wasn't like she had much choice, because my sister had made accusations against him concerning molestation. Some branch of the government responsible for overseeing the well-being of children sent a representative, and they informed my mother that Jack was not to be in the house under any circumstances.

After Jack was gone, my sister had started calling people, searching for my father. I never asked her why and she never explained. Joe (my father) was in Arkansas visiting, and he and my mother were talking about getting back together. I was stunned. It felt like the whole world had been turned upside down while I was sitting in a cage. Under other circumstances I would have been ecstatic, but right now there were other things on my mind. I'd given Deanna my word that I would find her, but time was slipping through my hands. I was beginning to feel that I would never again know what life was like beyond those walls. After being locked in a cage for weeks, the thought of ever getting out became one of those things that was too good to be true.

My mother and father came to see me the next day. There was no way to touch, and we had to talk to each other through two-inch thick bullet-proof glass. My father didn't even recognize me. When he and my mother walked through the door, I heard him ask her, "Is that him?" We were allowed to talk for fifteen minutes, them on one side of the glass and me on the other. That's not much time to get reacquainted, but my father promised that he would be part of my life from now on. The guard then came and told them it was time to leave.

I look back now and find myself filled with a tremendous amount of anger at how unjust it all was. The punishment didn't fit the crime by any stretch of the imagination. All I did was walk into an abandoned trailer. This made no sense.

A couple of days later Jerry Driver arrived once again, this time with my mother and father present. He needed a guardian in attendance to put me in the mental institution. I was given my clothes and told to get dressed. If you've never had to wear jail clothes, then you can't comprehend what it's like to finally be able to put your own clothes back on. It takes a while to get used to. The clothes are designed to strip you of any identity and reduce you to a number. You don't even feel like a human being when you have to wear them. You have no dignity.

The four of us traveled in Driver's car, and it was a long ride. It took several hours to get from Jonesboro to Little Rock, where the hospital was located. He restrained himself from asking more insane Satanist related questions in front of my parents, but I could tell it almost caused him physical pain to do so. Every time I looked up I saw his beady rat's eyes staring intently at me in the rearview mirror. For some unknown reason he had come to visit my mother while I waited in jail, and asked her if he could see my room. She let him in and left him back there alone. He told her that he was "confiscating" a few things, even though this was blatantly illegal. He took the Goya-like sketches from the walls, and a new journal I had started (It was in a funeral registry book, morbidly enough). He also took my skull collection.

It sounds kind of odd to have a skull collection, but it's easily explainable. There's a hard-packed dirt path behind Lakeshore that the local youth wandered on. It doesn't go anywhere specific, just sort of meanders around a small lake and a few fields. For some reason I always found odd pieces of skeletons that had died out there—possums, raccoons, squirrels, birds, and even the occasional dog or cat. I began collecting them because my teenage mind thought they "looked cool." I've never denied having questionable taste when it comes to interior decorating. The oddest thing we ever found was a beer bottle with two tiny skulls inside. The problem was that they were slightly too large to get out of the bottle. We spent hours trying to figure out how they got in the bottle in the first place.

At any rate, Jerry Driver took my personal possessions as "evidence." Evidence of what, he didn't say. I wouldn't know this for quite a while, as it would be some time before I ever saw Lakeshore again. For now, I was on my way to the funny farm.

◆   ◆   ◆

By the time we arrived, all the other patients had been put to bed. It was about ten o'clock at night and the place was completely silent. My mother and father sat in a small office giving my personal information to the woman in charge of filing paperwork on new patients. The process took about thirty minutes, and Jerry Driver sat silently listening to every piece of information. I was exceedingly nervous, having never been in such an environment before. The only thing I had to base my expectations on was the jail I had just left, so I was expecting the worst.

A nurse came to escort me through two large doors, back into the heart off the building itself. My mother was still answering questions as I left. Beyond those doors, it wasn't nearly as nice as the lobby we had just left behind, but it was also no chamber of horrors. All the furniture was made of a material similar to plastic, so that if anyone vomited or pissed themselves, there would not stain. It also possessed the added bonus of only needing to be hosed off after the occasional fecal smearing.

I was told to sit at a small table where I was introduced to a tall, thin, black guy named Ron. He looked through my suitcase, logged down everything I had, then showed me to a room. There were two beds, a desk, a chair, and a small wardrobe in which to hang your clothes. I was alone; there was no one in the other bed. I'd been through so much stress and trauma during the past few weeks that I immediately fell into a deep sleep which lasted until morning.

◆   ◆   ◆

The day began with a nurse making wake up calls at six AM. She turned on the lights and went from room to room telling everyone to prepare for breakfast. Everyone got up, took a shower, got dressed, and performs whatever morning rituals the insane carry out in privacy. You then march down to the day room, sit on the puke-proof couches, and stare at each other until seven o'clock.

On my first morning there were only three other patients. The first I saw was a blond haired girl who was sitting with her back to me and singing a Guns-N-Roses song. I looked at the back of her head for a while, until I became curious about what she looked like. When I could no longer take the curiosity I walked around in front of her. She looked up at me with ice blue eyes that seemed either half asleep or fully hypnotized, and she smiled. By her gaze alone you could tell that something just wasn't right with this picture. She seemed happy, and rightfully so, as she was being discharged later in the day. Her name was Michelle, and she was there for attempting suicide by swallowing thumbtacks and hair barrettes.

Soon a second patient entered. He was wearing Bermuda shorts and flip-flops, and could have easily passed for Michelle's twin brother. I never knew what he was there for, and he was discharged in less than three days. The third patient was a young black guy who seemed to be the most normal of the trio. He went home the next day.

If I had any fear of being left alone, it was soon laid to rest. Patients began to come in on a daily basis, and soon the entire place was full. I had to share my room with an interesting young sociopath who was sent there after being discovered at his new hobby—masturbating into a syringe and injecting it into dogs. The entire ward was a parade of bizarre characters.

We lined up every morning and strolled down to the kitchen for a tasty breakfast of biscuits and gravy, orange juice, blueberry muffins, hash browns, scrambled eggs, toast, sausage, and frosted flakes. The insane do not count carbs. The food was delicious, and I enjoyed every meal. Conversation around the table was never dull and covered topics such as who had stolen whose underwear, or whether or not Quasimodo had ever been a sumo wrestler.

Once breakfast was over we walked single file (in theory) back down to our wing and had the first of four group therapy sessions for the day. At this session you had to set a daily goal for yourself such as, "My goal for the day is to learn the rules," or "My goal for the day is to deal with my anger in a more constructive manner than I did yesterday." This made everyone irritable, because it's hard to come up with another goal every single day, and we couldn't use the same one twice. My last group was right before bed. I had to say if you had achieved your goal, and if not then why not.

Next came my weekly visit to the psychiatrist. We'd all sit on the couches and fidget while she called us in one at a time to talk. She had a small, dark, pleasant office filled with bookshelves. This was the doctor in charge of making your diagnosis and deciding what medication you needed. My diagnosis was depression. No shit. My life was hell and showed no signs of improvement, I had a stepfather who was a ten on the asshole scale, I'd just spent weeks in jail for reasons I still didn't understand, I didn't know where my lover was being held, and I was locked in a building full of sociopaths, schizophrenics, and other assorted freaks. You bet your ass I was depressed. I'd be more inclined to believe I had a problem if I wasn't depressed. At any rate, I was prescribed anti-depressants, which I was given starting that night.

Anti-depressants were a horrid invention. The only thing I could tell they did was make me so tired I couldn't think straight. I told one of the nurses that something was wrong because it hurt to open my eyes and I kept falling asleep every time I quit moving. I was told not to worry, this was natural, and I'd get used to it. That's not something you want to hear. Over time I did grow used to it, and in another month I wasn't even able to tell I'd taken anything.

After talking to the doctor, I went to the gym for a bit of morning exercise. There was a stationary bike, a punching bag, a rowing machine and a stair master. Everyone spent time on each one. There was also a foosball table and a basketball goal we could use after lunch.

Every so often we went to an arts and crafts room to work on individual projects. I made two ceramic unicorns that I took home with me when I left. I've no idea what eventually happened to them, but I was proud of them at the time.

For lunch it was back to the kitchen, then another group session, which was usually greeted with outraged cries of, "This is bullshit!" I agreed wholeheartedly, but kept my opinion silent. After suffering through this indignity, we were allowed to take a thirty-minute nap.

In the evening we went outside to a large fenced-in area to walk around and enjoy the air. We talked, looked out into the woods, or bounced tennis balls back and forth. Before bed we were allowed to choose a snack. There were granola bars, chocolate milk, peanut butter and crackers, or a cup of pudding. It wasn't a bad place to be, as far as psych wards go.

We were rewarded for good behavior by being taken on field trips. Once we were all loaded into a long, white van with a giant handicapped symbol on the side and taken to the circus. It was hard to tell if there were more clowns in the show or in the stands. Another time we were taken swimming. I never even got in the pool. I stood under an umbrella, dressed head to toe in black and waited to go back to the hospital. The last and most wretched trip was to a movie theater, where we watched Whoopi Goldberg in *Sister Act.*

Life went on, with my anxiety continuing to build. After I had been there for about three weeks my mother, father, and sister came to visit. A therapist came in with them to describe how and what I'd been doing over the past few weeks. Before turning to leave us alone she informed them that they could come to her with any questions they may have. This was the first real chance I had to talk to my father in many years, and we discussed both the future and the past.

He lived in Oregon now and had been preparing to go back when my sister had contacted him. He had been married several times since he left, and my eight-year-old half-brother now lived with him. I was amazed to learn that he and my mother would soon be married again, and as soon as I was out of the hospital, we were all moving to Oregon. Ordinarily I would have been thrilled, as this was everything I could possibly have wanted—Jack was gone, my father was back, I was receiving a twenty-four hour pass to spend the next day with my family, and we were moving up in the world—but now it was a nightmare. I was leaving Deanna behind. I started to rock gently in my chair as I silently cried. I didn't make a sound, but the tears came so fast and heavy that I couldn't see the room. I was looking at the world from behind a waterfall. I was sad and desperate, but something in my guts turned to steel. I knew I would keep my word no matter what.

I barely slept that night, thinking of the adventure ahead. This was a whole new life. I could leave my past behind like an old skin, something I would have previously given anything for.

When morning arrived, I got dressed and packed my things, because I would be staying in a motel room that night. I love hotels and motels. There's something exciting about it, even though you're only sleeping. I hadn't had a chance to do it in many years—not since before my mother and father were divorced.

They arrived to pick me up in my father's Dodge Charger, and I was impressed. Chrome mags, a nice paint job, and top-of-the-line-stereo system. I loved the car immediately. They asked me what I wanted to do, so we went to McDonalds, where I saw some people I knew. They were in the high school band and had some sort of competition in Little Rock, where by some amazing coincidence they had wandered into this very McDonald's. When a girl named Becky asked what I was doing there, I informed her that I was out on a twenty-four hour pass from the nearby mental institution. After she realized I was serious, she erupted into peals of laughter.

We got a motel room, and my father and I went down to rent a VCR and some tapes. We got every Steven Segal film they had and went back to watch them. He already had all of these movies at home, and they were some of his favorites. I enjoyed myself more that night than I had in a very long time, even though there were things nagging at me. We ordered pizza, watched movies, and talked about what it was like in Oregon. They tried to please me and kept the curtains drawn and the air turned low so that the room was like ice. It was almost as if today were my birthday. They knew I'd been through hell lately, and were being extra nice. I fell asleep early because I was still emotionally exhausted.

The next morning I had a breakfast of doughnuts before heading back to the hospital. Before they left, the doctor told my parents I would be discharged in twenty-four hours and they could pick me up. I never understood the point of having to come back for one more day, but it passed quickly enough. After saying goodbye to the other patients, I was on my way to Oregon.

XXI

The trip to Oregon took almost a full week and I enjoyed every moment of it, even with a sadness in my heart that felt like a weight. I was leaving my home behind and I was more than a little scared that I'd never see anyone or anything I knew ever again. I cried so hard I couldn't see the road until we were halfway through Oklahoma. I could tell it made my father nervous by the way he kept glancing at me out of the corner of his eye. After the first day I had exhausted my grief supply and could cry no more for the time being. That's when it became more fun.

The trip took so long because we made it in my father's car while pulling an orange U-haul trailer. We listened to music all the way, alternating between my father's collection and mine. The Eagles, Conway Twitty, and Garth Brooks was followed by Ozzy Osbourne, Anthrax, and Metallica, all played at ear shattering volume. We ate every meal at roadside places and slept every night in cheap motels. This was the life I had loved as a young child, when my mother and father were together, and we moved to a new state every month or so.

My father was in rare form throughout the entire trip, and I laughed at his insanity until I lost my breath. He spent all of one morning pointing out the prairie dogs along the side of the road and around rest stops. With a grave air and facial expression that said he was imparting divine wisdom, he explained that I should keep my eyes open because if I saw someone run over one of the prairie dogs, I would then see all its friends run out and start eating it. The manner in which he relayed this tidbit of knowledge that caused me to erupt into uncontrollable laughter. He looked at me for a moment before snickering, abruptly stopped, and his eyes darted around as if he feared someone might be listening in. This made me laugh even harder because I could tell he had no idea what I found so funny.

Watching my father interact with restaurant employees is an interesting and humorous experience in itself. It's hard to put your finger on specific things, but when looking at the overall picture it's hilarious. He'll order a cup of coffee and then look intently at the waitress as he emphasizes the words "two" and "sugars." She then turns to walk away and he'll call out to her with a "Hey!" When she looks back he makes direct eye contact while solemnly and slowly holding up two fingers as if to remind her—"two."

My little brother is a quandary too. It sounds odd if I say he was just like my father yet completely different, but it's true. His mannerisms are completely his own, yet everything he does seems like something my father would do. I lost all contact with him eleven years ago when he went to live with his mother, yet I still often think of him and wonder what kind of person he turned out to be.

We arrived in Oregon and moved into a three-bedroom apartment in a town called Aloha. It was a very nice place and I was given the biggest room, though I had nothing to fill it with. Unloading the trailer, I realized my mother had brought almost none of our belongings. I asked her where everything was, and she said she'd left it all in Lakeshore. This was almost impossible for me to believe. She didn't try to sell anything to get more money for the trip, she didn't even give it to others who may need it—she just abandoned it. The only thing of mine to be brought along was a single suitcase containing my clothes and music. This blew my mind.

When I later returned to Arkansas Jason told me he saw everything in the garbage. He was walking past one day and noticed everything I owned in one big pile by the curb—television, stereo, baseball bat, antique Japanese rifle, skateboard, electric guitar, and everything else that had been in the house. I asked him if anyone looked through it and took anything, to which he shook his head—"We figured it must not have been any good, or they wouldn't have thrown it away." Things we had spent a lifetime collecting were now gone as if never having existed. I would have been more upset if not for the fact that in two days I'd be starting a new job. I figured I'd soon be able to replace everything since I'd be working full time.

◆   ◆   ◆

My father was the manager of a local chain of garages and gas stations, so he gave me a job working for him. I would be bringing home well over 400 dollars every two weeks, and the job was easy enough. I was in a place where not a lot of traffic came through, so I and an old Vietnam War vet named Dave covered the shift by ourselves. We mostly sat and watched the traffic pass while sipping cold drinks and listening to country music on the radio. Dave was a cynical, cantankerous, old bastard, and he was the closest thing to a friend I had in Oregon. Despite our age difference, we got along quite well together. Most of Dave's vocabulary consisted of swear words, and he fired them like bullets at everyone and everything on earth.

Being that I now had a full time job, I was no longer in school. I never made the decision to quit; it was more like my parents made it for me. They didn't actually say, "You're quitting school," but they didn't have to. It was pretty obvious when they enrolled my sister and brother in a new school and didn't do the same for me. I was resentful but said nothing. At least I was making money now.

◆   ◆   ◆

When at home, my little brother began developing some odd habits. He watched *The Texas Chainsaw Massacre II* over and over, even though it scared him so bad he couldn't sleep at night. He mimicked characters from the movie and walked around the house scratching his head with a coat hanger while pretending to eat flakes of dandruff. He had a small plastic sunflower that wore sunglasses and a bow tie, and when placed next to a radio it danced to the beat of the music. He carried it everywhere with him, and as far as I know it was his only playmate. My sister began to hang out with some pretty shady characters and was always drinking or partying with them. This was the first time in her life she'd ever experienced any freedom, and she was taking advantage of it. When we were with Jack he'd rarely let her leave the house.

One day, after we'd been there about a month, I decided the time had come to shake a leg and get busy. My first order of business was to call Deanna's house. When her mother answered I had my sister ask for Deanna. The second she was on the line I took the phone and said, "It's me." Her voice sounded odd, almost like a little girl, when she asked, "Where are you?" I told her I was in Oregon, and asked if there was someone hovering around her, to which she said indeed there was. My heart sang just at hearing her, being in contact again. It was more than just her—I was talking to home, to my familiar world. I was on the phone with someone who didn't sound like they had a yankee accent. I felt alive again. I felt like myself, and that was a rare thing of late.

It's hard to describe what had changed. Ever since walking through the doors of that mental institution I'd felt like an old man shuffling his feet along the halls of a nursing home. Talking to her sent a wave of energy through me that shook the rust off and I felt ready to get moving again. That all ended in less than sixty seconds. "Do you still want me to come for you?" If she said yes, I would leave right then, even if I had to walk.

She didn't say yes, though. What she said was, "I don't know." Never had I hesitated when it came to her, and never had I doubted. To do so never crossed my mind, but I could hear it in her voice. She was hesitating, uncertain. The magick was broken. The last thing she ever said to me was "I have to go now." She hung up the phone and we have never spoken again to this day.

Up until that point my life had at least had a purpose, a direction, some part of me still had faith that it would all work out. That was now gone and I was infinitely tired. I'd put all my energy into this relationship and now had none left. I sat on the edge of the bed and stared at the wall for a very long time, not knowing what else to do.

My parents were going out of state to visit relatives in California, and were gone for a few days. While there, they picked up my grandmother, who was flying in because she didn't think she was strong enough to make the road trip to Oregon when the rest of us came. I chose to stay at home. Once they were gone, I walked to the corner store and bought two of the cheapest bottles of wine they had—Wild Irish Rose. I spent the entire night sitting out on the balcony looking down into the street and drowning my sorrows with the foulest tasting alcohol ever dreamed by man. I guess I was at the point which most people call "rock bottom." I was so lonely that I no longer felt like expending the energy necessary to keep living. When the sun began to rise I went to bed and didn't get up for several days.

Little did I know, Jerry Driver had been a busy bee in my absence. Deanna's reluctance came from the fact that Driver had told her parents that I was a Satanic monster and the head of a very large cult that was up to all sorts of skullduggery in the area. Driver had no doubt Deanna's life was in danger as there was no telling what foul plot I had devised to trap her in. He told them he was positive that I had been committing sacrifices all over town, that I'd been burning down churches (even though no church in the area was burned), and that I had a hand in infinite other untold crimes. He wove a tale in which I was the very incarnation of evil, come to create hell in Arkansas.

Why did he do this? I don't know. I didn't learn all these facts until much later when local teenagers said he questioned them about me every time they went out into the streets of Lakeshore, burning gas and taxpayer's dollars, as he terrorized young teenage boys. Many later said that he'd pick them up and threaten to take them to jail unless they performed sexual favors for him. He was beyond a doubt a very sick individual, but I never have understood why it was me that became his obsession. He once went so far as to make Jason take off his shirt so he could "inspect him for satanic markings." His life must have been pretty void while I was out of the state. I was also later told that he convinced Deanna's parent to send her to a "deprogramming center" to be certain she was no longer under the influence of my nefarious spell, and that they should contact him at once if they ever saw or heard from me again. That's precisely what happened.

After I got off the phone with Deanna her parents questioned her about the call and she eventually told them it was me. They called Driver and sent up a red alert. Driver's reaction was to call the police in Oregon and tell them that I was on probation in Arkansas for all sorts of satanic crimes and that I should be arrested at once. The police seemed to think it some sort of joke, but when he kept demanding that I be arrested for calling Deanna, they sent someone out to talk to me.

An officer in plain clothes came to our apartment to find out what was going on. He sat at the kitchen table drinking a cup of coffee as he asked me and my family questions. I told him that I had indeed called Deanna, but that I was no satanic kingpin and had no idea what Driver was raving about. The officer reported that I was breaking no law, didn't seem to be abnormal, and that the apartment was not the hot bed of satanic activity that Driver seemed to want them to believe. I can only imagine the tantrum Jerry Driver threw when they refused to obey him.

Meanwhile I became more lethargic and lackluster by the day. I no longer cared about anything. My mother expressed concern that I would harm myself, though I never seriously considered it. Everything exploded one night over a simple misunderstanding.

I had some Kahlua and planned to drink it in milk. I've never been a big fan of alcohol of any sort, but this stuff had a nice chocolaty taste and helped me to sleep. I poured it into the milk and stirred briskly. My sister went and told my mother that I was in the kitchen, "doing something sneaky." Of course I was being sneaky, I was trying to spend my dole money on the pint without being caught!

My mother didn't bother to come and ask me anything, she went behind my back and called a local mental hospital. As I was walking back to my room I heard her talking very quietly on the phone, so I stopped to listen. She was telling whoever was on the other end that I had been depressed and quiet lately, and feared that I may commit suicide. I couldn't believe what I was hearing. This was the lowest thing anyone had ever done to me in my life. This was betrayal of epic proportions. You must understand my mother to be able to really understand why she did this.

If you don't know her you could easily mistake her action for the concern of a caring parent. In reality it was the action of a drama queen. My mother loves to create drama, as I've already said. She still does. Every time a reporter comes around she can't keep her mouth shut and goes into her "poor mother" routine, complete with a copious amount of tears. I've seen it too many times.

I continued on to my room and listened to the radio for a few minutes, knowing she had set an unalterable chain of events into motion. Within a very short time, someone knocked on the door, and I opened it to discover a police officer. He asked if I would talk to him, so we took a seat in the living room. I couldn't believe the difference between the police in Oregon and the police in Arkansas. This guy was well-groomed and in shape, very polite, and could speak proper English. He treated me like a human being, and I may have even liked the guy under other circumstances. I agreed to go down to the place my mother had called because in the end I really had no choice. The cop left, and I got in the car with my parents.

The place turned out to be a small wing of a regular medical hospital, and I took a seat in the waiting room after we arrived. I sat there waiting to see a doctor and wondering why the hell this was happening to me. My mother has made more than her fair share of stupid mistakes, but I believe this one was the most ridiculous. My relationship with my father also changed this night.

It's been so many years that I can now no longer even remember exactly what was said, but it was something along the lines of, "You need to straighten up and fly right, I'm tired of you moping around all the time, blah, blah, blah." He followed it up with some kind of threat. He was trying to be a hard ass because I refused to speak to either he or my mother. I had nothing to say to them, not after doing this to me. I listened to his whole angry spiel without saying anything, but every word he spoke changed the way I saw him. It was as if I had a realization. Suddenly I saw my father not as a man, but as a boy. He was a child who had never lived up to a single responsibility in his life, and he had failed me in every way conceivable. He had abandoned me, left me to live in poverty and squalor with a hateful, religious zealot of a stepfather and a mother who wouldn't raise a hand to protect us from his tyranny. I saw him as weak, knowing he wouldn't have survived the despair of a life like he had left me to. I didn't want to hear anything else from him. With absolute contempt I spat the words, "I'd eat you alive." The prosecutor during my trail tried to say that I meant these words literally—that I was a cannibal lacking nothing but a bone to put through my nose. Of course I meant nothing of the sort, and only someone who was intellectually challenged would have dreamed up such an allegation. What it meant was that I realized I was stronger than my father, that I had survived a life I knew he would have crumbled beneath the weight of. I had survived without him, and he was doing me no great favor by being back in my life now. I was disgusted by his childishness.

When I finally saw a doctor he admitted me to the hospital and I was given a room. This place was nothing like the hospital in Little Rock, it was more like an asylum. There were no group therapy sessions, no interaction with staff, no scheduled routines, no anything. The patients spent all their time wandering the hallways, looking out the windows at the city below, or whispering among themselves. I didn't understand the point of being there.

My parents came to see me the next day, and my mother behaved in her typical fashion—as if all was now forgiven and we'd go back to being friends. Not this time. I was fed up with her. I told her that if she didn't check me out of this place immediately, then I never wanted to see her again. Her only response was, "If that's what you want," and they left. It was too much to ask that they stay away, and they returned once again the next day.

I was taken into an office to see a doctor, and my parents were sitting on a couch inside. I was in no mood to make friends, and behaved quite boorishly. The doctor finally asked me, "What is it you want?" Perhaps this is a question only a medical doctor has the intelligence to ask, because my mother and father certainly never did so. I no longer trusted my parents and could see only one option—"I want to go home." I didn't mean "home" as in an apartment in Oregon. When I said home I meant Arkansas. I didn't believe there was a chance in hell of it happening, so I was stunned when my parents agreed to it. Arrangements were made for me to be discharged the next morning, and I would take a bus back down south.

There wasn't much sleep for me that night. I went to bed but mostly just tossed and turned. I kept trying to form a plan of what I would do once I got to Arkansas, but couldn't keep my mind on it. I didn't even have a place to go once II got there, but I didn't care. I knew it would all come together in time. All that mattered now is that I would soon be back home. The month I'd been gone seemed like years.

At daybreak I showered, dressed, and ate breakfast. A security guard lead me downstairs and out the front door, where I saw my mother and father standing on a sidewalk next to a cab. My suitcase was sitting at their feet. My father handed me a bus ticket and the money left over from my last paycheck. I hugged him goodbye, but his body was stiff and rigid, as if he was reluctant to touch me. He didn't say much. Same with my mother. I put my suitcase in the cab and climbed aboard for the trip to the bus station. I was nervous, I was excited, and I was on my own at the age of seventeen.

◆   ◆   ◆

I'd never been on a bus before, so the experience was a little surreal. I had only been waiting in the station about fifteen minutes when the intercom announced that everyone should board now. My suitcase was placed in a storage compartment and I took an anonymous seat in the middle of a row.

As I watched the bus rapidly fill I noticed the passengers seemed to all have quite a bit in common. They were all unshaven and appeared to be in need of a bath, most were ill-tempered and barked out at anyone who got too close to them. Somehow all the dregs of society had found their way onto a single bus. It was the smelly, grouchy greyhound from hell.

I put on my most fierce facial expression in hopes of scaring away anyone who may be tempted to sit next to me. It seemed to work. No one had the inclination to sit next to a scowling creature with unbrushed hair and dressed in black leather.

The entire magickal voyage lasted for five enchanting days. We stopped mostly at gas stations and convenience stores for people to buy supplies, then we were be off again. I survived on a steady diet of chips and soda, with an occasional sandwich. Sometimes we stopped at a McDonald's for breakfast, but I never went in. I stuck close to the bus in a constant state of anxiety that it would leave without me.

On the second or third day I was reluctantly pulled into a conversation with two other gentlemen who had come aboard at the last stop. One guy was young, about nineteen or twenty years old, the other guy looked to be about fifty, but it was difficult to tell because of the layers of fat and road dirt. The young guy had long black hair and was wearing a leather jacket with a picture of Madonna airbrushed on the back. He spoke in a soft, quiet voice and chain-smoked clove cigarettes every time the bus made a stop. The old guy had a loud, obnoxious voice, greasy, grey hair, and was dressed in cut off sweat pants and a filthy teal colored shirt. He smoked cigarettes he rolled himself, and his hands were stained yellow from the nicotine. His fingers reminded me of some animal's horns. Being that I had nothing else to do, I found myself sitting with them whenever we had a layover. The young guy and I sat on the ground in what kids call "indian style," but the old man's legs were too fat for such maneuvering—he sprawled out, panting from the effort. He was a braggart who gave speeches on every topic under the sun, and you couldn't find anything that this guy didn't claim to know something about. There was nothing else of interest happening, so I studied him as if he were an obese ant farm. He was absolutely revolting, but you couldn't quit watching him.

They both set out to convince me that I should join them, working at a carnival that traveled from state to state. They spoke nonstop about the glories and riches I could acquire if I chose to undertake this noble profession. I thanked them, but declined the offer on the grounds that I was holding out for a more lucrative deal in the porn industry. Somewhere between Oregon and Missouri they departed the scene, and I continued my journey alone.

The longest layover was in St. Louis, where I spent six hours. I left the bus station to go exploring and stumbled upon an extraordinary number of dubious individuals. An old black man that looked like a fugitive from the intensive care unit tried to sell me drugs before I was more than ten feet away from the station. This was a neighborhood in which one definitely didn't want to be caught after dark, and since night was rapidly approaching I soon beat a hasty retreat back to the station. I spent the remainder of the time talking to a guy from Germany who had come to the U.S. in search of his father.

We crossed the Arkansas state line somewhere between two and three AM, but I still had trouble believing I was there. A part of me was certain the place no longer existed—that it had disappeared once I left. I looked out the window into the darkness beyond and kept thinking, *I'm back, I'm back, I'm back*—projecting it out into the night. It was Saturday morning, and everyone else on the bus was asleep. I couldn't sit still. Every landmark I recognized pushed me to a new level of excitement. When we passed the cemetery where my grandfather was buried it took all my self-control not to tell the bus driver, "I need off *now*! Let me out *here!*"

We pulled into the bus station just as the sun was rising. No one else stirred; I was the only one getting off. Getting off the bus, I retrieved my suitcase and looked around. Everything I could see looked exactly the same as when I left.

XXII

I was stopped by a cop less than ten minutes after getting off the bus. There was no one to pick me up, so I was going to have to walk while carrying my luggage. The closest person I knew was Domini, and she lived about three miles away. I thought that perhaps I could leave my suitcase there while searching for a place to stay, so that's where I started off to.

As I crossed the street from the bus station a cop car pulled around the corner. I was greeted with flashing blue lights and a blaring siren. I have no idea what I did to "arouse his suspicion," but he pulled up next to me and rolled down the window. Behind the wheel was an insolent slob with a stomach so huge he could barely squeeze into the front seat. With a voice somewhere between a hare-lipped drone and an obnoxious whine, he began to ask, "What's your name? Where are you going? Why are you dressed like that?"

I had broken no laws and was doing nothing wrong. He was harassing me simply because he could. The only reason he eventually left me alone was because he got a call on his radio. If not for that, there's no telling where the situation would have went.

Walking three miles with a large, heavy suitcase took forever. I had to stop every so often to rub my hands, which were quickly developing blisters. This short jaunt took an eternity, and the day was rapidly growing hot. Summers in Arkansas are brutal, and this morning was going to be a fine example. When I reached the apartment complex where Domini lived I was exhausted and covered in sweat.

I had an odd sensation as I made my way between the buildings. It was a complex mixture of thoughts and feelings, one of which was amazement (and perhaps pleasure) at how nothing had changed. The only difference was the way I now saw everything. When I had come here to see Domini in the past, I was always struck by how different this place was from Lakeshore. Then again, Lakeshore is different from every other place. I was sleep deprived and hungry, and I couldn't decide which was more dreamlike—the time I'd spent in Oregon or being back here now.

My feelings about West Memphis and Arkansas in general have always been something of a paradox. The people here have often been cruel and hateful towards me, and I've been so lonely that I thought the envy would kill me. I didn't fit into the social scenes, and there aren't many opportunities to be had here, but it's been my home. The place itself is alive with a kind of magick that can cause my heart to feel like it's bursting. There is a scent in the air I can't describe. I wish everyone who reads this could feel it just once. You would remember it forever.

When I stepped in front of Domini's apartment she was on the second floor looking out an open window. She glanced down and saw me, looked shocked for a second, then disappeared back into her room. A few seconds later the front door came open and Domini ran out. All she said was, "Hi" when she hugged me. She felt familiar to me in her own way, but there was no power or passion to it like there was with Deanna.

The word I associate with Domini is just "pleasant." Hugging Domini is pleasant. I told her I was back for good and asked if I could leave my luggage there until I figured out what I was going to do with it. She helped me get it inside and out of the way, then said she'd come with me to Lakeshore. My next step was to let Jason know that I was back.

As Domini and I walked the mile or so to Lakeshore, I told her all about my having been sent to the hospital, the return of my father, and the great Oregon adventure. She was explaining that she would let me stay with her if it wasn't for her aunt and uncle's objections when a cop stopped me for the second time that day. It wasn't even lunch yet. He pulled up next to us, got out of his car, and struck a pose like some sort of obese superhero. This one asked all the same questions the first one did, and I had to go through the same routine. The most obnoxious thing was the way he acted as if he was entitled to know my business.

As a child, I was taught in school that living in America automatically entitles you to certain freedoms, yet the older I've gotten the more I've come to know the harsh reality. These cops could stop me anytime and anywhere to make demands of me that I had no choice but to comply with. Even though I was doing nothing wrong, I was forced to tell them where I'm going, where I'm from, and any other personal information they demand of me, all because they don't like the way I look. The only freedom I had was to obey or go to jail. They never taught me that in school.

When this ass clown finally released us, we continued on to Lakeshore. I hadn't realized how much I'd missed that dilapidated hellhole until I saw it again. That trailer park was a magickal place. I still miss it now, even though the Lakeshore I knew is gone. The scummy green water and the dead fish smell in the air said "home" to me like nothing else.

As Jason's trailer came into view, I wanted to break into a run. I knew he'd still be sleeping, so I slapped the window next to where his head would be. He peeked out the window looking irritated and half asleep, then realized who it was and quickly ran to open the front door. He was highly excited and ushered us inside where he was the only one home. Once we were all seated, I had to explain again where I'd been and what had happened. I hadn't seen Jason since he'd left Deanna and I in the abandoned trailer that afternoon, so the whole thing had been a mystery to him.

He told us how he'd knocked on my door one day to discover a whole different family inside, and none of them had ever even heard of me. It was as if I had disappeared from the face of the earth without a trace, and he was certain he'd never see me again. When I told him about Oregon he just shook his head and said, "I would have never come back." I'd have said the same thing myself before I had the experience.

We discussed the fact that I didn't know for certain where I was going to stay yet, and agreed how great it would be if I could stay with him. We both knew his mother would never agree to it, but later that day he tried to convince her anyway. As we expected, the idea was met with much hostility.

My only real option was Brain. I made the trip to his house accompanied by both Jason and Domini. He started laughing the moment he opened the door and saw who it was. We all sat on the patio, and I explained for the third and final time where I'd been. Brain was more amazed than I expected him to be, which resulted from the fact that he thought I had still been around and had simply dropped out of sight for a while. He found the entire story to be very amusing and laughed as if my misfortunes were the epitome of stupidity and hilarity. My life had taken on the quality of an episode of *The Three Stooges* in his eyes. He asked questions when he wanted me to clarify certain points, all the while staring at me like he couldn't believe what he was hearing.

Brian had a plan that was both simple and ingenious—I would stay with him, but we would tell no one. As long as his mother didn't know I was living in the house, she could not object to it. I was impressed with his logic. After much pleading and cajoling, we convinced his brother to drive to Domini's and pick up my suitcase, although he seemed none too fond of the idea of me living with him.

The weekend was a flurry of excitement because I was so happy to be back and around the people I knew. We talked about what I missed while gone, drove around Memphis like old times, got reacquainted with people I'd forgotten about, and generally enjoyed ourselves. I slept on Brian's floor Saturday and Sunday night, then on Monday morning I went with him to school.

Attempting to enroll myself in school turned out to be one more thing on a long list of disappointments. The principal informed me that I needed a parent present to sign me up because I was not yet eighteen years old. I explained how this was impossible as both of my parents were now living on the other side of the country. There was nothing he could do and suggested that I consider getting a GED instead. I found the idea to be distasteful, but I could see that I was making no progress in pleading my case. Dejected, I returned to Brian's house where I ordered a pizza and watched television for the rest of the day.

When Brian returned home from school, I told him what happened and we put our heads together to form a solution. In the end, the conclusion we came to was that we'd have to see if the school would allow his mother to enroll me. We never had a chance to test this plan and school would soon be the least of my worries. The very next day would find me back in jail.

XXIII

Tuesday morning Brain got up and followed his usual routine of preparing for school. I was jealous that he got to go and I did not. I loved going to school, I just didn't like doing the work. I always thought school was more fun than a carnival. Everyone I knew was going to be there, so the day was impossibly boring for me during school hours.

Brian left, and I settled in for another long day of watching television. When lunchtime came, I ordered another pizza. I knew I couldn't eat the food in the house or Brian's mom would become suspicious. I was pretty sure I could live on pizza until my money ran out, then I'd have to think of something else.

Twenty minutes after I placed my daily pizza order there was a knock at the front door. Thinking that my provisions had arrived I opened the door to discover Jerry Driver and one of his two cronies. Driver was trying his best to look official, and had a pair of mirrored sunglasses stretched across his rotund face. His partner was a skinny black man who one day met the wrong end of a shotgun after sleeping with another man's wife.

"I'm here to arrest you," Driver wheezed.

This was quite a shock to me, as the only crime I had committed was not being in school, and that was not for lack of trying. "For what?" I asked him.

He began stuttering as if I had caught him off guard with such a question. His jowls quivered as he managed to insult my intelligence with the crime of being under the age of eighteen and not living in the household with my parents. I seriously doubted his assertion that this was a criminal offense, but I once again had no choice in the matter. I was forced to wear chains and shackles as if I were a dangerous, hardened convict, while Driver ushered me back to the jail I had previously been in.

This time Driver's questions became even more bizarre and outrageous. I was taken into a small office and chained to a chair as he and the black guy tried to entice me to read texts to them that were written in Latin. He showed me odd objects such as glass pyramids and silver rings with strange designs. He wanted me to explain the significance of these items to him. I had not the slightest clue what any of it meant, but he refused to accept that answer. When he was finished with this, I was left in a jail cell for a few more weeks.

I knew what to expect this time, but that didn't make the ordeal any less horrendous. The endless days in a cage, the fights that erupt all around you, the inedible gruel, the humiliating orange clothes, and the way the jailers treat you like scum—it all comes together to create an incredible mental pressure that's maddening. You feel defeated and hopeless. What made it even worse is that this time I knew I had done nothing wrong. I was being punished at the whim of an obsessive, delusional, power hungry liar. I just couldn't figure out why this clown had become obsessed with me.

After my time in jail I was once again sent back to the mental hospital in Little Rock. Jerry Driver took me himself, as he had obtained a court order for my institutionalization. I was chained and shackled for the entire trip. When we arrived, the other patients were quite disturbed by the sight of me. They later confided that they had believed I must be a madman of the highest order to require all the restraints. You know you've hit rock bottom when mental patients question your sanity.

Luckily, I only had to spend two weeks at the hospital this time. During my first conversation with the doctor she said, "I have no idea why they brought you back here, because I see no reason for it." It would have taken too long to explain Driver's fixation, so I just shrugged my shoulders as if to say, "I don't know why you're asking me, I only live here." I was kept two weeks just for the sake of following procedure, and then I was discharged. On my last day I said goodbye to all the other patients, some of whom I really liked. There's always a huge emotional scene anytime someone is released.

I walked to the front desk and saw that I was being picked up by none other than Jack Echols. Jerry Driver had contacted him while I was hospitalized, told him where to pick me up, and said that I was his responsibility since he had legally adopted me. If I had a choice I would have checked myself back into the hospital. Unfortunately, I didn't. I would now be living with Jack Echols again. I was caught in an endless cycle of hell.

XXIV

Living with Jack was worse now than ever before. I could tell he really didn't want me there but felt like he had no choice in the matter. While I had been in Oregon he had been renting a small room that was barely bigger than a closet, so he had to find a new place once he found out I would be coming back. That place was a tiny trailer in Lakeshore. It was barely big enough to stay out of each other's way.

Unsurprisingly, Jack didn't have a single friend in the world. Every moment that he wasn't at work was spent in a chair in front of the television. Other than yelling at me, the only topics of conversation he employed were about how my sister had ruined his life by telling social services that he had molested her, or how wrong my mother had treated him by filing for a divorce. He was sickening to me, and I hated the very sight of him in his sweat stained shirts.

He went to bed at eight PM every night, which meant that I was forced to do the same. After eight o'clock I was not allowed to turn on a light because he said it kept him awake, so there was no reading. I couldn't watch T.V. or listen to the radio—not even a walkman. He claimed that he could hear it playing in his room even with the headphones clasped firmly to my ears. I couldn't go out after six o'clock because he would have to sit up and let me in. When I asked why he didn't just give me a key, he said because he wouldn't be able to fasten the chain lock, and I'd wake him up coming in. He had three locks on the door and still felt the need to prop a chair against it every night so that no one could break in. The only thing a thief could have taken was the jar of pennies next to Jack's bed or the huge picture of Jesus hanging in the living room. Only a true crackhead would break into that place.

Jack Echols is always angry. Sometimes it's at a simmer, other times he erupts into a screaming fit, but there's always anger. I couldn't tiptoe around him or stay invisible in such a tiny place, so his rage was always directed at me. He did nothing but sit in his chair stewing and brewing, filling the rooms with misery and hatred. It was unbearable. Brian had moved to Missouri the day after I got out of the hospital, so my only refuge was Jason's house. I slept there as much as possible.

Jerry Driver had also told Jack that he wanted me to check into his office once a week for reasons unknown. The first day of every week I made the five-mile trek to Driver's office where he and his two side kicks (Jones and Murry) questioned me. Their approach no longer seemed friendly. They had switched tactics and become downright antagonistic. Most often Driver and I were alone, but if one of the two others were there they'd appear to be deep in thought while Driver asked one question after another about Satanic activity.

During the winter months and rainy days, Jack didn't work nearly as much, so he took me to Driver's office. As long as Jack was present, Driver refrained from his usual insanity. His beady eyes gleamed and his whiskers twitched as he stared at me across the desk, but he managed to restrain himself. After Jack came with me every week for over a month Driver must have grown exasperated thinking he'd never again be able to see me alone. Admitting defeat, he said I no longer had to check in.

While Jason and Domini were in school, I had nothing else to do but read. I educated myself since I couldn't go to school. I spent most of every day in the West Memphis Public Library, devouring book after book. I loved that library. There's something a little creepy about all that knowledge housed in one place. It gives the books a slightly sinister aspect.

I eventually took my old principal's advice and got my GED. I was hoping I'd have to attend classes or something, but no such luck. I scored so high on the pre-test that I was immediately given the real thing and passed with flying colors.

Being that I was still on the antidepressants given to me during my first visit to the hospital, I had to make periodic visits to a local mental health center. This is where a doctor would refill my prescription. They never bothered to check and see if I actually needed them, I'd just be handed a prescription like it was a hall pass.

I thought my life was pretty dull, but Jerry Driver must have believed otherwise. One day Jason and I were sitting in Jack's trailer watching television while he was at work. I answered a knock at the door to discover one of the local Lakeshore youths named Bo. He was sweating and breathless as he came in and helped himself to a soda before telling me that Driver was around the corner at the Lakeshore store asking questions about me. "He asked me which street you lived on and I said I didn't know," Bo informed me without a trace of irony in his voice. Driver had also told everyone at the store to stay away from me because sooner or later I was "going down," and anyone with me would meet the same fate.

Upon hearing this news Jason looked at me with an aggravated expression on his face and said, "What the fuck are we doing? We never do anything, but this freak is telling everyone we're running wild. Doesn't he have any real crimes to solve?" Apparently not.

The last time I saw Driver before my trial was the night of the high school homecoming football game. Jason and I went to it because there was absolutely nothing else to do. We had to walk home after it was over, which is when we were intercepted by my old friend Jerry Driver. He was riding up and down the streets of Lakeshore, probably looking for me. He asked where we were going, what we were doing, etc. When he finished the interrogation we continued on our way to Jason's trailer where we passed the night watching horror movies. I forgot all about this incident until I was on trial for murder and Driver testified.

He told a great many lies, some of which were that Jesse Misskelley was walking with us, that we were all three carrying staves and dressed in Satanic regalia, and that he believed we were returning from some sort of devil worshipping orgy. The jury ate it up like candy and loved every sordid detail. A story straight from the tabloids, right next to "Bigfoot Sighted!" or "Bat Boy Born in Cave!" This was evidence.

The misery of living with Jack reached a fevered pitch when I also had to work with him. He decided that I should have a job and that I was incapable of finding one for myself. The truth is that it's almost impossible to convince someone to hire you when you don't have a car or anyone willing to drive you. I had tried everywhere. Jack convinced his boss to hire me to work alongside him doing roof construction.

The job was hard, boring, and dangerous, but the worst part was that I never had a second in which I was out of Jack Echols' presence. We got up at sunrise and didn't get home until nightfall. The only thing I could do was come home, eat supper, go to bed and rest for the next day. I was chained to him day and night, there wasn't one moment when I was free of him. This went on for months. I began to hate my life and could easily see myself trapped forever. Jack became more of a bastard by the day, and it wasn't just me that noticed it. The people we worked with tried to be friendly to him and were met with hatefulness.

I grew more and more desperate to escape his presence. I wracked my brain attempting to come up with an idea that would allow me to break free. Finally I discovered the answer, which Jerry Driver himself had handed to me. He had insisted that I be confined to a mental institution on two separate occasions, and now I took advantage of it.

I went to the Social Security office and applied for disability benefits. They looked over my application, which detailed my stays in the hospital and declared me mentally disabled. I was entitled to a check every month. I wasn't allowed to work and draw the check at the same time, so this was my escape from working with Jack. The chain was broken. When I told Jason about it he laughingly said I was receiving "crazy checks." The name stuck, and that's what we came to commonly refer to my income as. "Have you gotten your crazy check yet?" Yes, indeed.

◆   ◆   ◆

My grandmother and grandfather on my father's side of the family moved to West Memphis, and I began to spend time at their house. I kept my grandmother company while my grandfather was at work. I dearly love my paternal grandparents. No matter how old I get I always feel like a kid around them. To have that feeling around anyone else would be irritating, but I didn't mind it at all around them. It made life seem clean and simple. You can't stay in a black mood when visiting my grandmother; it's impossible. Jason usually went with me because he knew there was always food there. As soon as we walked in she began preparing huge bowls of chili for us, or bacon and eggs with toast, sometimes pork chops or fried chicken. Dessert was always Dolly Madison cakes and ice-cold cans of Coke. My grandmother is a saint.

One day while visiting her, my mother called. My grandmother told her that I was there visiting and then handed me the phone. I talked to my mother and father who were both still in Oregon. It wasn't unpleasant; they mostly asked what I was doing, where I was staying, how Domini and Jason were, etc. I had my reservations, but didn't mind talking to them. It became a routine that when I was at my grandmother's house I'd speak to them on the phone. We were getting along, but I remained wary of them to a certain degree, like a dog that had bitten me in the past.

Domini now skipped school more often than not, and stayed with me while Jack was at work. We never had a burning romance, but we kept each other company. I had no desire to get into another situation where I risked the sort of trauma that I had experienced with Deanna, and Domini was safe. We were friends who had sex, and that's the only type of relationship I was willing to have then. Perhaps that makes me sound selfish, but I will be nothing if not truthful. My worst fear in the world was having my heart broken. When she called me one day and said to come over I already knew what was happening.

I knew exactly what she was going to say once I got there, but curiously I felt nothing. I knew my life was about to change forever, yet I was strangely detached.

I wasn't especially happy, nor was there sadness to speak of. There was neither excitement nor dread. I was Zen master for a day.

When I arrived Domini was smiling, glowing. She had an assortment of papers scattered across the kitchen table and her mother was with her. The papers were medical pamphlets. I sat in a chair; she sat on my lap and put her arms around my neck. She said the exact thing I knew she was going to. She told me she was pregnant.

XXV

My eighteenth birthday came and went on silent feet. There was no cake, no celebration, no well-wishers. Jack didn't even remember it, or if he did made no mention. I'm certain his hatred of me equaled my disgust with him by this point. Having me in his house was a reminder of his failed relationship and disgrace. At least I was now officially an adult, and out of Jerry Driver's realm of manipulation. He was a juvenile officer, which meant he was only allowed to harass children.

Domini's aunt and uncle had decided to move, and were leaving her and her mother behind. Domini's mother was in extremely poor health. She was diabetic and needed insulin injections, not to mention the fact that the left side of her body was almost completely paralyzed due to a stroke. It took her ten minutes to walk the length of a room, and she often needed help getting dressed. Needless to say, the doors of opportunity weren't exactly banging open for her.

After searching for a place to stay, they located a rapidly disintegrating trailer in Lakeshore. They had procured a van to move their things, but a 100 pound pregnant girl and a half paralyzed woman proved to be less than adept at the moving process. In the end most of the loading and unloading fell to me, but I really didn't mind. It gave me a chance to look at all the interesting things they had accumulated, and there were quite a few. They were more than a little worried about how they were going to make ends meet.

Meanwhile, pressures continued to mount with Jack. He constantly accused me of things I hadn't done, such as having parties and letting people go into his room while he was at work. I didn't know enough people to put together a party, and there was nothing in his room worth going in there for. He ranted and raved, screaming at me, pressing his face right into mine, but he drew the line at hitting me. I could tell he sometimes wanted to, but he never did.

Late one night I could take it no more. He was bellowing at me as usual when I simply got up and left. I walked out while he was in mid-tirade.

It was dark, cold, and drizzling as I walked up and down the streets of Lakeshore. It seems it's always cold, dark, and drizzling when I go through momentous emotional changes. I used to wear an old, black slouch hat, and I liked to watch the rain drip off the brim. It made me feel like a character in a spaghetti western. That's what I did for a couple of hours before finally going to Domini's, where I slept that night.

I went and got my things the next day while Jack was at work and brought them back. Between my "crazy check" and the money Domini got from her father, we managed to pay rent and survive. We even started buying a few items for the baby we would soon have. We couldn't afford a car, so a decent job remained beyond my grasp. I was certain that if I just had a way to get across the bridge to Memphis every day I could find something good.

Domini quit high school because of the pregnancy, and we spent the days together. We went on walks, watched television, fed the ducks who came to the lake, or kept her mom company while listening to music. We passed the days in this fashion for several months. We talked about what we should do once the baby was born and agreed that we should get married, although we never laid solid plans.

I continued talking to my parents on the phone, and not long after I told them Domini was pregnant, they told me they were moving back to Arkansas. It seems that things weren't going so well for them in Oregon. I wasn't certain how I felt about this, because I knew it meant they'd be back in my life. Could be good, could be bad. Time would tell. They would be here in about a week or so. I told them our address so they could come see us once they were in town.

These calm, quiet, uneventful months with Domini was one of the times I allowed myself to be lulled into a false sense of security and fell prey to the belief that things would never change. It wasn't that I wanted things to remain that way forever, it just seemed that I didn't have much choice in the matter. I was wasting away. Ever since I was a child, I'd felt like I was doing nothing but waiting for my special place in life to be revealed to me. Often I was frightened that I'd miss it when it did. I felt that the stagnant life I was living was not what I was destined for, but had no idea what to do about it. All I could do was wait, wait, wait. I knew I wasn't meant to live and die in a trailer park the rest of the world had never even heard of.

XXVI

My parents arrived in Arkansas early on a week day morning. Domini and I were still in bed sleeping when my mother and sister knocked at our door and Domini's mom let them in. I could hear them talking in the living room and figured I'd better get up. If anything, my mother's southern accent seemed to have deepened while she was away. It was very odd hearing her voice in person again; it made the day seem special somehow, like a holiday.

I deliberately took my time getting dressed and brushing my hair before going into the living room, mostly because I didn't know what to do. I had no idea how to behave in this situation. When I finally entered the room, I saw my mother and sister in chairs, my sister was wide-eyed but silent. My father wasn't there. I wondered to myself if that meant anything. My mother turned to see me looking at her, then quickly bustled over to hug me. The first thing that struck me was how much I'd grown. I now stood a full head taller than her. While my mother theatrically shed the few requisite tears I hugged my sister and asked where my father was. He was at their new place, unloading their things. My little brother was with him. He met us at my paternal grandmother's house for breakfast.

Domini and I both went with them and listened to tales of their adventures in Oregon on the way. They seemed to be well rested and cheerful despite their weeklong drive. When I first laid eyes on my father he was transparent, I could read him quite easily. I could see something like doubt in his face, as if he were much like myself in not knowing what to do. He was nervous and uncertain.

Not having a clue what to say, I hugged him. Domini did the same. That seemed to put him at ease, the awkwardness faded away, and he began behaving like his normal self. The single most familiar thing about my father to me is his cough. He coughs a great deal because of his life long smoking habit, and hearing him cough put me at ease for some reason. It softened my heart towards both of them. Perhaps because it reminded me that they were both only human, subject to the same failings as everyone else. My mother had gotten pregnant at the age of fifteen, they were both high school dropouts and had never known any other life.

At least I was capable of knowing there was some other kind of life possible, even if I was having trouble achieving it. They believed that the way they were living is the only kind of life that existed. They had no imagination to envision anything else, and no desire to reach it. I felt sorry for them. I still do sometimes, although that doesn't mean their constant idiocy isn't capable of driving me to the brink of madness. They never have learned from their mistakes. It would probably be easier on everyone if I stopped expecting them to.

After they had settled into their new place I began spending time with them. I alternated between the place with Domini and my parents' place. Sometimes Domini did too, and Jason was known to stay over. One day he laughingly called me a nomad after we made stops at both places, then traveled to my grandmother's to see what tasty dishes she would serve. Once he mentioned it, I did feel like a bit of a gypsy. I didn't quarrel with my parents after that, maybe due to the fact that I could always escape them.

XXVII

I was now legally an adult, an expectant father, and in a relationship I was certain would end in marriage. I would never have abandoned Domini, as I take my responsibilities seriously and feel disgust for those who don't. Sometimes I think that comes from sheer determination not to make the same mistakes my father did. Still, I was not in love. I still thought of Deanna pretty frequently, wondering what had happened. I never feel that I can move on in life unless I have closure for the previous stage. It never comes in the form I expect and often leaves me feeling empty.

Through sheer coincidence (I use that word but don't believe there's any such thing) I found out where Deanna's family had started attending church. The possibility of seeing her again plagued me. I couldn't drive it out of my head. I constantly wondered what would happen, how she would react, what I would see in her eyes, and a plethora of other questions I needed answers to. I couldn't understand how she had so thoroughly and completely severed our connection. I needed an explanation. I knew there was no chance of talking to her, but I couldn't help but feel that I could learn something just by seeing her eyes, her face. I needed that ever-elusive sense of closure.

Sunday morning found me preparing to descend into the hellish realm of fundamentalism. From the outside the church looked like a Kentucky Fried Chicken shack with a steeple. I knew I didn't belong there, but I had to do it or I would get no rest. Slinking inside I took a seat on the very back bench and watched the activity. People obnoxiously called out greetings, shook hands, and slapped one another on the back as if they hadn't seen each other in years. I saw people glance at me from the corner of their eyes, but no one approached me. No one smiled at me, shook my hand, or slapped me on the back. No one even said "hello."

Scanning the rows, I saw Deanna sitting in the dead center of the room. Her entire family was alongside her. I hadn't seen her in a year, but she hadn't changed at all. I'm not sure what it was that I felt, but my heart was in my throat. I couldn't breathe. She looked at me, and looked away. I didn't even see a flicker of recognition. What did that mean? I had been expecting something, anything—but her eyes passed over me as if I were not even there. I sat through the entire hour and a half of the red-faced preacher bellowing and beating his fist against the podium, but never heard a word of it. I stared at Deanna's back, willing her to turn around and give me some sort of reaction, but she never did.

When it was over, I walked outside and stood on the sidewalk. I was trying to figure out what this meant as I watched her family get in their car and drive away. I turned to leave and heard someone call out, "Hey! I want to talk to you for a minute!" he was staring at me without blinking as he approached.

He stood before me with crossed arms, not offering to shake my hand. "What's that?" he asked, pointing to a pin on my jacket. It was the iron cross from the cover of the Guns-N-Roses *Appetite for Destruction* album. "That some sort of Satanic thing?"

I told him it most certainly was not, but he still looked dubious. "I don't want you coming here making people uncomfortable." He looked like he was working himself up into a state of anger. "Don't worry, I won't be back." I walked away still trying to figure out what it all meant.

XXVIII

I've nearly come to the end of my tales as a free man. This last section of the story has already been chronicled by two documentaries, two books, hundreds of newspaper articles, a few short stories, and will soon be the focus of a movie. All of those views come from the outside of the looking glass, so I'll attempt to describe what it was like from this side.

Domini and I had been arguing a little, though nothing serious. It was mostly in the vein of people of who have spent too much time together and just need a break. I had slept at my parents' house for the past couple of nights to create some breathing space. One morning I got up, and with hair still tangled I went out to have a nice big bowl of Fruitloops for breakfast. Toucan Sam makes a mean box of cereal. While I was happily munching and contemplating the fact that I would soon have a bowl of pink milk, I flipped on the television. Nothing goes better with Fruitloops than cartoons. There were no cartoons this day. I went through every channel, but it was all the same show. It was special news coverage of three kids who had been murdered. It looked like every reporter in the world had descended upon the town of West Memphis.

It wasn't just the T.V. that was talking about it—the whole town was abuzz. It was the conversation on everyone's lips. I truly don't believe there was anyone not talking about it, and the rumors were already starting to fly. I heard the same two words countless times over the next month—"Satanists" and "sacrifice." Every day that passed without anyone being arrested only made that conclusion grow more and more firm in the minds of every gossipmonger in town.

The very same day I saw the first news coverage is when the police began to sniff around my door, although they later denied it and said they never considered me a suspect until several weeks down the road. Not long after the coverage began, a cop named Sudberry and one of Jerry Driver's sidekicks, Jones, came knocking. I found it interesting that Jerry Driver himself didn't show up. They came into the house and said they wanted to talk to me privately. Evidently they did not want my family to hear what they had to say. My mother, sister, and paternal grandmother watched as I lead Sudberry and Jones into a bedroom and closed the door. They sat on the edge of the bed, one on either side of me.

This was the first time I'd ever seen Sudberry. He was potbellied with a horri-ble comb-over and had weak, watery eyes. He also sported the mustache that only cops and gay porn stars from the 70s seem to like. He didn't say much, and just sat quietly while Driver's cohort asked the questions. Jones was all saccharine and lying eyes as he said things like, "Something bad has happened, and we really need your help." Instead of questioning me about the murders he stayed on top-ics such as, "What's your favorite book of the bible, and why? Have you ever read anything by Anton LaVey? Who is your favorite author?" It seemed they couldn't choose between conducting a murder investigation and filing a book report. Of course eventually came the inevitable, "Have you heard anything about devil-worshippers in the area, or any plans to sacrifice children?" To be quite honest I found it sickening. Instead of attempting to find out who had murdered three children they would rather indulge in these childish fairy tales and grab-ass games. A fine example of your tax dollars at work.

Before leaving they took a Polaroid picture of me. Later I found out that they showed it to nearly everyone in town, using it to plant ideas in the heads of an already frightened public. In court they denied taking the picture or ever even coming to see me that day. They had to, because Jones and Driver were from a different office and weren't supposed to be involved in the investigation in any way. By that point the blatant lies no longer shocked me because I'd seen it too many times.

This visit was not a one-time occurrence. They were soon coming at me every single day. They came to my parents' house, to the place Domini and I stayed, and to Jason's house. It wasn't always the same two; there was a rotating crew of about six of them. It the same questions, day after day. It became pretty apparent that these clowns weren't looking for a murderer. Jerry Driver and his two cohorts put a bug in their ears, and they couldn't shake it. Instead of conducting this like a real murder investigation and checking the forensic evidence, they were chasing stories of black robed figures who danced around bonfires and chanted demonic incantations. Soon that's all anyone could talk about. The entire town was petrified because they were convinced hell had broken loose in Arkansas. Every redneck preacher in the area was preaching sermons about how we were in the "end times" so you'd better get right with God or else the devil would come for you, too. You must keep in mind that this is a state in which one out of every four people can't read above a fifth-grade level. Ignorance breeds superstition. They literally believed these stories, and helped them to grow. After being shown my picture one man swore to the police that I caused him to levitate. Another swore that the police told him that they had found body parts under my bed. These sorts of stories passed for investigation.

The constant harassment continued to escalate. Soon instead of coming to my house they were taking me to the police station. Here it was easier for them to play "good cop/bad cop." One of them (usually Sudberry, whose breath smelled as if he ate onions morning, noon, and night) got in my face and scream, "You're going to fry! You may as well tell us you did it now!" The other cop would then pretend to be my friend and act as if he were rescuing me from Sudberry's "wrath." I was only a teenager, and the whole thing looked pretty pathetic even to me. This continued day after day for a month. My grandmother grew worried and sold her rings to hire an attorney to come to the police station with me, but the police refused to let him in. They lied and said I never asked for him, even though I did so several times. My grandmother lost her engagement ring and wedding ring for nothing.

I didn't think there was anything wrong with answering their questions, because I had nothing to hide. I had done nothing wrong, and figured they would sooner or later get this insanity out of their system. It didn't work that way. The more I cooperated, the more abusive and belligerent they became.

The last time I went into the police station before the arrest I was kept for eight hours. I was not allowed a drink of water, a bite of food, or even to use the restroom. They screamed and threatened me the entire time, trying to force me to make a confession. The psychological pressure was enormous. They would have kept me all night if I wouldn't have finally demanded they either charge me with a crime or let me go home. I suffered from extreme exhaustion, my head was pounding, and my body kept trying to vomit, although there was nothing in my stomach. I felt like I'd been run over. If you've never been through anything like that, then there's no way you can understand. There's no word that fits what they did to me other than torture.

Late one evening my mother, father, and grandmother left to go to a casino for a night of gambling. My grandmother loved playing blackjack more than just about anything else in the world, and my parents were more than happy to keep her company at the table. They would be gone all night. I, my sister, Jason, and Domini all settled down for an evening of watching horror videos. We were making fun of a movie that seemed to have been put together with more imagination than money when someone started beating on the door. Not knocking, but literally beating. You could feel the vibration through your feet on the floor. The beater screamed, "This is Sudberry, open the door!"

My first thought was "To hell with that." I was sick of these ass clowns tormenting me day after day. I figured it was more of the same and that they'd eventually get tired of waiting and leave. When the beating continued and grew even more persistent I knew something wasn't right. They were being even more aggressive than usual. I went to answer the door to see what they wanted.

When I opened the door there were three cops on the steps, all pointing guns directly at my face. The barrels of the weapons were less than three inches away from touching my skin. Another cop was standing on the ground pointing a gun at my chest. Sudberry nearly tackled me in his eagerness to handcuff me and get me into a cop car. Looking over my shoulder I told Domini, "Don't worry about it." After all, it's impossible for them to prove you've done something you haven't done, right? At least that's what I thought.

I didn't see them arrest Jason; I was rushed out too quickly. I later found out they took him out right after me. After I was put into a car, I was driven straight to the police station and escorted to a small office by a cop that looked disturbingly like a pig that had been taught to walk upright. I never saw a single cop in the station who was even close to being physically fit, but this guy was the worst of the lot. He was so fat he was suffocating under his own weight. He weighed at least 350 pounds. He had no neck, and his nose was turned up like a snout. I've learned over the years that sooner or later a persons' physical appearance comes to resemble whatever is in their heart. I shudder to think what this guy's true nature was. For some reason I couldn't stop thinking of him as "Piggy Little."

Piggy Little was an old school asshole. You could tell he'd never succeeded at anything in his life, and he was out for revenge. He seemed to think his personal God-given mission in life was to harass and torment me in every way possible. Perhaps I looked like someone who had stolen one of his Twinkies as a kid. Whatever the case he felt like he had to keep his sausage-like fingers on me at all times so that he could push, pull, and shove me.

Eventually the head cop of the station came into the office and sat behind a desk. His name was Gitchell, and I'd seen him at the station a couple of times before, but I'd never had to deal with him. Now he wanted to have a conference. Gitchell was slightly more intelligent than his coworkers, which is most likely why he was the boss. He was no intellectual giant, but he didn't have to be when compared to the rest.

"Is there something you want to tell me?" he asked.

I stared at him blankly, saying nothing.

"You may as well tell me something now because your friend has already confessed. This is your only chance to make sure you don't take all the blame." I felt like I had somehow gotten lost in this conversation, or that I must be missing something, because it wasn't making sense to me. Friend? Confessed?

"Who are you talking about?" I asked. It was his turn to look at me blankly. I had no idea who he could be talking about, because I knew it couldn't be Jason.

He continued along the same lines with statements like, "You should just tell us something, because your friend is already pointing the finger at you. If you want to make sure he doesn't put everything on you this is your only chance." This went on for at least half an hour, Gitchell talking while Piggy glared. When he finally realized this wasn't going anywhere I was put inside a cell that wasn't much larger than a phone booth. I was left there throughout the night, confined to a space so small I couldn't even stretch my legs out. There was no water, no restroom, no anything. Every so often Gitchell came in and ask more of the same. Once he came in and said, "One of the officers told me you wanted to talk to me." I hadn't even seen an officer in hours. "He lied," I informed him. This continued until well after sunrise.

When I wasn't being questioned I was constantly trying to solve this mystery. Who could Gitchell be talking about? What had he said I did? None of it made any sense.

A cop came in and demanded my clothes. I'd never experienced anything like this in my life and thought him some sort of pervert, judging by the looks of him. When I was given more clothes it was an old, ragged police uniform that was at least twelve sizes too large. It looked like they had brought me a pair of Piggy's pants. I had to gather the waist and tie it into a knot to keep them from falling down. This is how I made my first court appearance.

I was taken through a narrow hallway through the back of the jail. When it suddenly opened up into a courtroom I was stunned, because of the contrast. The jail itself was filthy and roach infested to the point of making you not want to touch anything for fear of contamination. It was a place the general public was never meant to see. I'd grown used to seeing that, so the dazzling clean and well-lit courtroom was jarring.

I blinked like an animal pulled from its hole and looked around me. The place was packed from wall to wall, and the only faces I recognized were my mother and father. Everyone else in the place seemed to be shooting daggers of hatred at me with their eyes. Every few seconds someone popped up like a whack-a-mole game and snapped pictures of me. I hadn't slept in about thirty-six hours, so everything had a slightly surreal quality to it.

The judge began rambling while I leaned against a wall to keep my knees from buckling. Four cops kept their hands on me at all times, as if they expected me to break and run at any second. When the judge got to the "How do you plead?" part of the show, I said, "Not guilty." My voice sounded flat, dull, and small. I felt a wave of outrage directed towards me from the peanut gallery. The judge's droning sounded strangely like an auctioneer as he began talking about a confession. I was so exhausted and in shock that I could follow very little of what he was saying. It finally dawned on me that he was asking if I wanted the confession read out loud or just entered into the record. Starting to feel a little pissed, my voice was a little more forceful this time as I said, "Read it." I could tell he didn't like that idea at all. As a matter of fact he seemed down right uncomfortable as he looked down and started shuffling papers.

Finally he stuttered that he wasn't going to do that, but that he would call for a recess until after I had read it. During the recess I was taken into a broom closet filled with cleaning supplies, and was handed a stack of papers while two cops stood staring at me. My brain was so numb that I could only comprehend about one fifth of what I was reading, but at least now I knew who had made the confession. The name at the top was Jesse Misskelley. My first thought was, *did he really do it?* followed quickly by, *why did he say I did it?* Even in my shell-shocked state I could tell something about this "confession" wasn't right. For one thing, every line seemed to contradict the one before it. Any idiot could plainly see he was just agreeing with everything the cops said. That's when I knew why the judge didn't want it read out loud. Anyone with an even average I.Q. could see it was a setup. The whole thing seemed shady.

I'd always been raised to believe the cops were the good guys, and that dirty cops were few and far between. So why was no one stepping up to expose this for the bullshit it was? Why were they all going along with something so fraudulent? The answer: to save their asses. It seems quite a few of the cops there were already being investigated by the FBI for various forms of wrongdoing, and the last thing they needed was the entire world watching them as they bumbled around ineptly, pretending to conduct an investigation. They needed to put an end to this case quickly. As one of the cops told Jason—"You're just white trash. We could kill you and dump the body in the Mississippi, no one would care." We were throwaways, sub-humans. Feed us into the meat grinder, and the problem goes away. It's not like we were ever going to amount to anything anyway.

After I read the script/confession, I was taken back into the courtroom. The judge was rambling again, and I was on the verge of collapse. Suddenly everyone sprang to life as an overweight man with bad skin jumped from his seat and tried to run down the aisle. He was screaming something incoherently as the cops tackled him and I was hustled from the room. I later found out that he was the father of one of the murdered children. I couldn't really blame him. I have a ten-year-old son of my own, and I think I may have done the same if I thought I was looking at the man who had harmed him. He just needed someone to blame, to take his grief out on. He wasn't interested in facts or evidence.

Once back into the dark and dingy part of the building they began putting chains on me. Around my waist, my hands, my feet, and anywhere else they could think to attach them. I saw Jason a few feet ahead of me, and they were doing the same to him. He was also wearing one of the old, ragged uniforms. In front of him was Jesse Misskelley. He was wearing chains, but he had on his own clothes. Perhaps this was another small way of punishing Jason and I for not doing as they wanted.

They rushed Jesse through a door, and outside I saw sunlight and heard the roar of a crowd. It sounded like a referee had made a really bad call at the Superbowl. Next they carried Jason and me out at the same time. There was a circle of cops around me, all trying to drag me. I had to run to keep up with them, but there were chains on my legs and I had no shoes. They dragged me across the concrete, ripping off two of my toenails and a fair amount of skin. The crowd went into a frenzy at the sight of us. It looked like the entire city turned out to see us, and they were all screaming, yelling, and throwing things. They wanted to crucify us right then and there. I imagine this is the closest thing a modern man can come to knowing what it was like in the Roman Coliseum.

I was tossed into the back of a car and told to stay down. There were two cops in the front seat, both fat and wearing the standard 70's porn mustaches. They could have passed for brothers. The one behind the wheel quickly started driving at a high rate of speed. I was curled into the fetal position on the back seat, vomiting and dry heaving. One cop looked back at me, cursing and swearing. In disgust, he spit, "That's just fucking great." No one said another word to me for the rest of the trip, and I had no idea where I was going.

When we finally came to a stop sometime later in the afternoon it was at a small white building with several cop cars around it. A few old, crusty looking men were using a water hose to half-heartedly spray at the cop cars. As I was being escorted inside, I heard the cops tell them to wash out the back seat where I had gotten sick.

Once inside the chains were removed and I was told to strip. I stood naked while one cop sprayed my entire body with some sort of anti-lice spray. Four or five other cops looked on while conversing nonchalantly. This was nothing new to them. Soon enough I myself began to view such events as nothing out of the ordinary. After my flea dip I was given a pair of white pants and a white shirt to put on. One of the old, crusty car-washers from out front handed me a towel, a blanket, and a mat like preschoolers sleep on. The induction ceremony being complete, I was pushed into a cell that would be my home for most of the next year.

XXVIV

The area I was confined to had four concrete slabs that served as beds. There was a small metal table bolted down to the floor, a shower stall, and a television suspended high in one corner that could only pick up two channels. For the first week or so there was only one other person in the cell with me. His name was Chad, and he was there on a capital murder charge. He'd shot someone with a sawed off shotgun while burglarizing their house. Chad was a white guy with a terrible case of acne and unwashed curly hair. His back had already started to curve into a hump, like an old man, even though he was only sixteen.

Chad seemed a bit slow in the thinking department, if you catch my drift. He claimed he had been there for years, and was quite excited that he now had company. He couldn't answer a single one of my questions: he didn't know where we were, or how far from West Memphis I was, or how to make a phone call, or anything else I could think to ask him. He'd just smile really big, throw his hands up in the air as if to say, "Who knows? Only the gods can say." Then he would rock back and forth for awhile. Not so encouraging. My thinking was that perhaps my whereabouts were being kept secret from everyone, including Domini and my family. I was worried about how Domini was taking it. My family and I weren't always on the greatest of terms, but when you're drowning like I was, you'll reach for anything. I was lost and alone and empty. Floating deep in outer space could have been no more frightening. I had done nothing to deserve this, and I was goddamned if these assholes were going to make me the sacrificial lamb.

I was still taking anti-depressants, which the guards gave to me every night. I had the ingenious idea of saving them up and taking them all at once. That was the only way I could see out at this point. This situation was only getting worse and worse. There was no Sherlock Holmes coming to solve the case and let me out. Besides, what did I really have to live for, anyway? The only thing I would regret was not being here for the baby. It would have been nice to stick around for that.

When I was in the hospital I had heard that 800 mg of this particular medicine was enough to put you into a coma you'd never come out of. I wanted to be certain I did it right, so I took 1200 mg. I swallowed the pills and sat down to write a quick note for Domini and my family. It was only a few lines scratched out quickly with a pencil. That being taken care of, I stretched out on my concrete slab and flipped through one of Chad's magazines. He wasn't much of a reader, but he loved those pictures. He wasn't too fond of losing the only company he had, either. I hadn't bothered to hide what I was doing from him, thinking there was no need.

The main sensation I had was of being so tired that it was physically painful. I wanted to sleep more than I'd ever wanted anything in my life. I closed my eyes and just let go. That's when all hell broke loose. About ten guards came for me. Chad had told them what I did, because he didn't want to be left all alone again, especially with a dead body. I could hear them talking but couldn't make my eyes open. Someone opened them for me, and shined a flashlight in them. Someone else poured a vile tasting liquid in my mouth and was telling me to swallow it. It was some sort of vomit-inducing syrup. They put me in the back of a car and drove about 150 miles an hour to get me into a hospital. By this point I was so confused that I kept asking myself if the drugs were taking effect yet, or if I was already dead. I tried to tell the cop behind the wheel that we would have been there by now if we'd all ridden on the back of a giant spider. Unfortunately, my mouth didn't work the way I wanted it to.

I don't remember much about the hospital that night. I woke up for a moment when someone put a tube up my nose and down my throat. Two cops were sitting before me, watching, while all the doctors and nurses were moving double-time.

Can't let the star of the show die, can we? Strangely enough, all the doctors and nurses looked like therapists from the mental institution. I was awakened a couple of times during the night by someone shining a light in my eyes and asking if I remembered my name, but I slept through the entire stomach pumping procedure. When I finally woke up sometime the next day I found myself in the intensive care unit.

My lawyer first came to see me while I was in the hospital. He only stayed a few minutes, long enough to introduce himself and tell me my family knew where I was being held. He looked incredulous when I told him I was innocent.

I only saw him about three more times over the course of the next year, and never longer than thirty minutes. You would think that if a guy were going on trial, and could very well be sentenced to death, that his lawyers would spend a lot of time preparing him for court. Mine did not. I had never dealt with lawyers or court systems before, so I didn't know what to expect. Perhaps this is how capital cases are handled. After all, this guy is a lawyer, so he must know what he's doing, right? Surely they wouldn't appoint me a lawyer who was ineffectual or uncaring. I had a lot to learn.

The same court that was putting me on trial was also paying my lawyer. Look at it this way—are you going to employ someone who makes you look stupid and rubs your face into your own mistakes? No. You're going to pay the guy who knows his place and sticks with the program. These guys know they get paid the same amount whether they win or lose, so why try too hard? Later, during the trial, when I asked why they didn't push a point or challenge a ruling, they answered, "We have to work with the judge on a daily basis and don't want to piss him off."

"Beyond a reasonable doubt" disappeared and "Innocent until proven guilty" left the building. Once they go through all that trouble to get you, you're going down unless you've got a couple million dollars on hand to hire some real gun-slingers to come to your aid. I was a fool back then though, still wet behind the ears. I thought the point of the justice system was to see that justice be done. That's the way it always works on TV. While I was counting on divine interven-tion they were plotting my demise.

◆   ◆   ◆

Once I was released from the hospital and taken back to the jail, I was put in a padded cell with no clothes. I'd heard of padded rooms all my life, and imagined them to be like a giant pillow. It's nothing of the sort. Everything is coated in a thick, greasy substance similar to rubber. More like a bicycle tire filled with cement than a pillow. Since I had no clothes, it was pretty chilly. One of the guys passing by slid me some "National Enquirers" under the door. I read them dur-ing the day and covered up with them at night. There was nothing else to do in there. It was just an empty room.

There was a small opening in the door, and sometimes one of the other pris-oners on the block sat by the door and talked for a while. Everyone on the block, with one exception, was a young black guy who had already been to prison at least once in the past. The only exception was an old man in his fifties. His hair was as white as his skin was black, and all the other guys abused and took advan-tage of him. He was given absolutely no respect. He came sat by my door and cried for half an hour at a time, like I could help him somehow. He was there for having two children with his own daughter. He was their father and grandfather at the same time. He tried to stay quiet and out of everyone's way, but it didn't always work.

I spent a week in the padded cell, talking to people through the opening in the door and freezing. Contrary to what I had been led to believe by movies and T.V., none of them seemed like hardened criminals who would kill their mothers for a nickel. Some of them were pretty funny. Every night after lockdown someone called to the guy in the next cell, "Hey man, come here a minute, I need to show you something." There would be laughter, then "Shut up, fool, I'm trying to sleep." Several times a day someone beat on my door and asked, "You alright in there?" Their constant antics kept me from feeling quite so sad, at least until the lights went out. Once the lights went out and everyone was in bed, the despair came back full force. I cried myself to sleep many nights.

When I got out of the padded cell a week later, I was taken back to the cellblock with Chad. He was as pleased as could be, because counting myself he now had three roommates. While I was gone two more guys had come in. Both were black teenagers, one named James and one named Nikia (everyone called him Kilo). He turned out to be the second best friend I've ever had in my life. This guy was really smart, and extremely funny. We often said the same thing at the same time, or when I tried to explain something he would get excited and say, "Yeah! That's it exactly!" He slid across the cellblock floor on his knees doing a flawless Michael Jackson impersonation, and I laughed until my sides hurt.

We got a chessboard from somewhere, and I taught him the game. After playing several games a day for about a month, I could never beat him again. He kicked my ass at every game, unless we played "speed chess." This was a variation game that I invented, and its purpose was to prevent you from thinking about your next move. Your opponent had until the count of five to move a piece, or you could legally start thumping him in the forehead. It was a very fast five count, which gave you slightly under two seconds to grab a piece and move it.

Chad's family brought him some more games, so the four of us passed the time playing monopoly, checkers, chess, and dominoes. We all pooled our money, so that even the person with the smallest amount wouldn't have to do without anything. If my family left me twenty dollars, I'd buy twenty dollars worth of candy and chips, which was considered to belong to all of us. Kilo, Chad, and James did the same. We never had a single fight, which is a very rare thing when you've got guys who are forced to be in each other's faces twenty-four hours a day.

The guards at this place (the Monroe County Jail) were different from any I've ever seen since. These people were nice, polite, well groomed, and not abusive in any way. I was fooled into thinking all guards were this way. I didn't realize I was experiencing a miracle. They treated us like human beings, and even let us do things the other prisoners didn't get to do, like stay up all night. The four of us never went into the cells, we made small pallets on the day room floor, and lived like we were having an external slumber party.

Kilo and I both looked with great anticipation to Saturday at midnight, when a show called *Night Fright* came on. We were so starved for music that we'd listen to anything, and this was our only fix. It wasn't the music either of us preferred, but it was all we had. You never know how much you need music until you don't have it. I missed it so much my heart hurt.

◆   ◆   ◆

My mother, father, and Domini came to visit me once a week. We were allowed twenty minutes, and had to talk through bulletproof glass. Domini had been almost five months pregnant when I was arrested, but you still couldn't tell it by looking at her. In the last three or four months of the pregnancy she grew at an alarming rate. Her entire body was the same size it had always been, but her stomach became huge and tight. I wouldn't get to be there for the birth of my son. That was one more thing taken from me. A guard stuck her head in the door one morning and told me that I was now a father. So much for a celebration.

We had a boy, who is now nearing his eleventh birthday. Domini gave him my first name, only spelled differently—Damian. I gave him the middle name of Seth, which is what everyone calls him. We gave him a third name, Azariah, just to be certain he'd never have an inferiority complex. I wasn't there to sign the papers, so he has Domini's last name. She brought him to see me for twenty minutes every week, but I couldn't touch him.

They brought me five paperback books from a local second hand bookstore every week, and I'd usually have read them all by their next visit. I had always loved reading, but it now took on much more importance. Those books became my only way to forget about the nightmare of my life. I hid in them and went someplace else for hours at a time. The other guys were amazed by how much and how quickly I could read. It's a trend that has continued to this day. I've read a few thousand books over the time I've been locked up. Without books, I would have gone insane long ago. I adore them, and would love to one day have my own second hand bookstore. Learning has become my passion.

The only people to do any work on my case during this time period were two private investigators from Memphis named Ron Lax and Glori Schettles. Ron hit the streets and came up with useful information on an almost daily basis. Unfortunately, my lawyers (I was given two) used absolutely none of the information he found. They didn't even call the witnesses who could have testified to my whereabouts on the night of the murders. They never attempted to prove my alibi.

Glori came to see me nearly every single weekend, and always brought pizza. You could tell she really cared about this case, because she and Ron both went to tremendous effort even though they were never paid a penny for it. On my birthday, Glori even brought me a box of cupcakes. We sat alone in a small office eating cake and going over the case. She gave me hope.

About a month before my trial, I was transferred to a jail in the town of Jonesboro. It was nothing like Monroe County. The guards were all unnecessarily cruel and abusive. They talked to you as if addressing a lower life form, no matter how polite and civil you were to them. I witnessed them beat prisoners on an almost daily basis. About two weeks ago I was lying here in my cell watching the news when it was announced that five guards had been fired in Jonesboro because they had handcuffed a prisoner and beat him unconscious. They were fired. No charges were filed against them. Most of the time they're not even fired if they're caught, only demoted in rank. That's because prisoners aren't considered human to society at large. If you walk up to a man on the street and punch him in the face you go to prison for assault. Do the same thing to a man in prison and you get demoted. They had a small Mexican guy in jail there who suffered from catatonic schizophrenia. He sat or stood in an odd position for hours at a time due to mental illness. The guards beat him just to see if they could make him move. It was like a game to them. They often spit in your food to see if they could get you to fight. If you even say anything to them they'll call in five or six of their friends to beat you. Once you're behind the walls there is no help. The world doesn't care.

In Jonesboro, I was put in a cellblock by myself. There was no one to talk to, no books to read, no television to watch, and no going outside. I was locked in an empty concrete vault all day and night. I knew Jason was in the next cellblock, because I could hear the guys on that side through the wall. He was on a block with about ten other people. It would have been a huge comfort to be able to sit in the same room with him and carry on a normal conversation, perhaps try to figure out what went wrong, but the guards made certain we never even saw each other.

I gradually slipped deeper and deeper into depression and despair. When you're in total isolation there's nothing to take your mind off your fears. I had also recently heard the results of Jesse Misskelley's trial/circus. He had been found guilty and given one life sentence plus two twenty-year sentences. Life plus forty. It wasn't the death penalty, but it amounted to the same thing. Without a miracle he would die in prison. Jason and I were scheduled to go to trial together, though the attorneys were all fighting tooth and nail. It seemed like the entire world was howling for my blood.

XXX

The first morning of our trial, Jason and I were given bulletproof vests to wear to and from the courthouse. Emotions were running high and the cops were taking no chances. We arrived at court everyday in a convoy of police cars—about six of them, to be exact. When we pulled up out front, we had to walk a gauntlet. There was a huge crowd of reporters, and people who wanted us dead, and we had to walk right through the middle of them like Moses parting the Red Sea. The screams of hatred were so loud you couldn't discern individual voices. It was like fighting your way through a black wall. Reporters shoved cameras and microphones into your face at every step, all shouting questions at once.

Another interesting thing began to happen as the days progressed. People who supported us, and believed in us, began to trickle in one or two at a time. They smiled or gave me a slight nod as I made my way in or out. They were mostly young boys or girls standing apart from the rest, many dressed in black. I started to receive little bits of poetry scratched onto scraps of paper. Someone sent me a single red rose. The supporters never matched the haters in number or volume, but it mattered a great deal to me. There were a few odd cases, too. Ron started a ritual of pointing out the girls he said were "eye-fucking" me. As I got out of the car one morning a girl screamed, "Oh my god, he looked at me!" like she had just seen John, Paul, George, and Ringo rolled into one.

The reporters were the worst. If people knew how much of what they read in the papers or saw on the news is distorted or outright lies, media corporations would soon go out of business. I've seen more fiction on local news broadcasts than I've read in novels. Quite often, the newspaper accounts didn't match anything I saw go down in the courtroom. Valuable information went unreported. During a post-trial hearing, new evidence was presented—they had found teeth marks on one of the bodies, and they did not match my teeth. There was no mention of it in the next day's paper.

It's maddening to sit there hour after hour, day after day, on trial for something both you and the cops know you didn't do. You can feel hundreds of eyes drilling into you, taking in your every shift and move. Many seemed to think this was the greatest form of entertainment they'd ever witnessed. Vultures were stripping the flesh from my bones while I was still alive.

I never stood a chance. During breaks the judge and prosecutors told jokes about me and smiled like they were awaiting a pat on the back. The judge commented on what a nice ass one of the female potential jury members had, and the prosecutor's teeth stuck out while he yuk-yuk-yukked it up. Convincing twelve people they should vote to have me murdered was just another day at the office for them.

Whenever evidence was introduced that could have helped me, the jury was escorted from the room so they wouldn't hear it. The stepfather of one of the children was discovered to have a knife with blood on it that matched at least one of the victims. We were not even allowed to ask him, "Did you murder those children?" in the presence of the jury. Why? Because he wasn't the one on trial here, I was. It wasn't really a trial. More like a formality to get out of the way before the guilty verdict.

It would be redundant to go over every detail, because the world could view the whole thing by renting a DVD. With the rise of the internet you can even go online and read all the paperwork. I've never actually seen either a DVD or the Internet, but I've heard of such things, even in here.

We were both found to be guilty. I didn't need to call a phone line psychic to see that coming, but it was still crushing to the spirit. Perhaps it's human nature to clutch at any little bit of hope you can conjure up. I did, all the way to the very last second. It's devastating, even when you see it coming a mile away. When they read the verdict, I heard Domini start sobbing and run from the courtroom. I couldn't turn around to look, because my legs would have buckled. I was determined not to let them know how bad they were hurting me. I refused to give them that satisfaction. I would not cry, I would not faint, and I would not show weakness. I had to hold myself up by placing my hands on the table, but I tried to make it look casual. Inside, I started to die. There was no safe place in all the world for me. My stomach was filled with ice water. Hearing Domini was the final straw. Something in me was broken. All the King's horses and all the King's men would never be able to put me back together again.

I was sentenced to death, Jason to life without parole. After the reading of the sentence I was immediately rushed out of the courtroom and to a waiting car. As I was going out someone screamed, "You're going to die!" Someone else screamed, "No you're not!" The car door slammed, and we pulled out of the parking lot. I was on my way to death row.

XXXI

To get from the courthouse to the prison took about three hours. That's an eternity to a man who doesn't know what kind of situation he's walking into. Everyone in jail has horror stories to tell about prison. A lot of people think jail and prison are the same place, and that they know what the penitentiary is like because they were once picked up for being drunk. Jail is pre-school. Prison is for those earning a PhD in brutality.

My mind was numb and I couldn't think. I now know this was a combination of shock and post traumatic stress disorder—the same thing experienced by soldiers who have been in a fire fight. I shivered uncontrollably, though I didn't feel the cold outside. My life was over. That's the closest thing I could formulate to a thought. My execution date was set for May fifth. That was a couple of months away. The attorneys had told me don't worry about that, your first execution date means nothing. Everyone gets one of those, but getting a stay of execution is automatic. I'd like to see how well they laughed it off if it was their names on a piece of paper with a date next to it. Har har har, you jokers. That's a good one.

Most people who go to prison first make a stop at what is called the diagnostic center. That's where they give you a complete physical and mental evaluation. If you're going to death row there's no layover at the diagnostic center. What was the point? Physical and mental health don't really matter if you're standing before a firing squad. My trip ended at the bighouse itself.

It was dark outside when we pulled up, but the place was still lit up like a Christmas tree. The lights are never turned completely off in prison, and there are searchlights constantly moving to and fro. I was taken out of the car and into a small building where I was strip-searched and given a pair of "prison whites." That's what they call the uniform you're issued.

There was some fat clown in polyester pants, a short-sleeved shirt, and clip-on tie issuing orders. His air of self-importance led you to believe he was a warden or something. He had a horrendous little boy's haircut and the requisite 70s porn mustache. He was not the warden. In truth, he was assigned to the mental health division and had no authority whatsoever.

That's a common thing in the prison industry. They take some loser who has spent his life bagging groceries or asking, "Would you like fries with that?" and put them in a polyester guards uniform, then the would-be losers blow up like a puffer fish and march around like baby Hitlers. This is the only place they can feel important, so they fall in love with the job. It becomes their life, and they'd rather die than lose it.

The ass clown screams in my face, "Your number is SK931! Remember it!" I happened to glance at a digital clock that read 9:31 P.M. I wondered if everyone's number was the same as the time they came in (It was just a very bizarre coincidence). A nurse checked my temperature, blood pressure, and heart rate. They seemed to find it hilarious that my pulse registered like a rabbit in a snare.

After they finished, they took me to a filthy, rat-infested barracks that contained fifty-four cells. This was death row. You'd be amazed at how many letters I get from people saying they're sorry I'm on "death roll." I always picture that thing alligators do when they grab you and start spinning around and around. It rips you to shreds and drowns you at the same time. The death roll. I was put in number four call, and immediately fell asleep. I was exhausted from the trauma. Shutting down was the only way my mind could preserve itself.

◆   ◆   ◆

My first two weeks on death row were spent vomiting and sleeping. I was suffering a pretty fierce withdrawal from the antidepressants I had been on for three years. The prison system spends a bare minimum on medical care for inmates, so there was no way in hell they were going to pay for a luxury item like anti-depressants. Instead of gradually lowering my dosage the way it should have been done, I was forced to quit cold turkey. My sleep was troubled and I couldn't keep anything in my stomach. Even though it was agony, in hindsight I see that they were doing me a favor. I haven't been on any medication in over ten years, and I've never felt physically better or mentally clearer. I also lost all the weight I had gained while sitting in the county jail. You don't get much exercise when locked up in a cage, so I gained over sixty pounds by the time I went to court. I lost that and more. At one point I was down to 116 pounds.

When I arose from my concrete slab to begin my first full day of prison life, I noticed someone had dropped a package in my cell. Opening it, I saw that it contained a couple stamp envelopes, pen and paper, a can of shaving cream, a razor, a chocolate cupcake, grape soda, and letter of introduction. It was from a guy upstairs named Frankie Parker. No one called him by that name, though. Everyone called him either Ju San or Si-fu. He was a Zen Buddhist, and was ordained as a Rinzai Priest before his execution. That's where the name Ju San came from. Si-fu is a generic term that means "teacher" in Chinese. He was a huge white guy with a shaved head and tattoos of Asian style dragons on his back. The package he sent was something he did for every new person that came in, to help them get on their feet.

His constant companion was a guy that greatly resembled a cave man. His name was Gene, and he had dark hair that reached the small of his back and a full beard that reached his chest. Gene was a Theosophist, a follower of H.P. Blavatsky.

They both loaned me books on Buddhism and Theosophy, and answered countless questions. Listening to them debate each other in the yard was like watching a tennis match. Both of them lit a fire in me which grew into a decade long educational process. I made my way through texts such as *The Tibetan Book of the Dead* and *Isis Unveiled.*

These two guys were no dry scholars. They loved to laugh, and nothing was more hilarious to them than the perverse. They were completely irreverent. It was not unusual to hear one or the other make comments such as, "I like the way your butt sticks up in the air when you bow to that little Buddha statue." Gene was a remarkable painter, and I once saw a canvas he had painted to look like a giant dollar bill. If you looked closely you noticed it wasn't George Washington's picture in the middle, it was Jesus. Look even closer and you realized Jesus has a penis for an ear. He then lectured for an hour on what such symbolism meant. Believe it or not, I actually learned quite a bit from him.

I also learned quite a bit from the guy in the cell next to me, though I've never put such knowledge to use. He was an old biker from a gang called the Outlaws—rivals of the Hell's Angels. 300 pounds, blind in one eye, and barely able to walk, he was a horrendous sight. He was the epitome of hateful, old-age cunning. He was too old to fight, so he devised other ways to get revenge on those who did him wrong. He was known to befriend his enemies and then feed them rat poison and battery acid. A guy once stole five dollars from him, then found himself on the floor puking up blood after drinking a cup of coffee. He told me everything I needed to know in order to move and operate within the system. He also sold me my first radio. After not hearing music for the past year, Lynyrd Skynyrd sounded like a choir of angels.

After I'd been here a few weeks I started to get requests from media sources, asking me to do interviews. I thought that this could be my chance to tell my story to the rest of the world. It was obvious that no one else was going to do it for me. So, I granted a couple interviews, with disastrous results. A local news station got hold of the footage of one of my interviews and claimed I had talked "exclusively" to them. In truth I never talked to anyone from their station, they only cut and spliced the footage to make it appear that I had done so. A newscaster said something like, "Here's Damien Echols, talking about his leadership of a Satanic cult!" They then showed clips of me speaking about something completely unrelated to anything they had said. That wasn't the worst part, though. The worst was when the prison administration decided to teach me the folly of my ways.

◆   ◆   ◆

People in prison have their own language, and it takes awhile to grow accustomed to it. For example, "shoot me a kite" means don't discuss business out loud, write it down and pass it to me. "Catch out" means shut up and leave or violence will soon follow. "Reckless eyeballing" means you're looking at someone a little too closely. "Ear hustling" or "Ear popping" means someone is trying to listen in to your conversation. "Shake down" means the guards are coming to destroy your cell in a search for contraband. A shake down is how my "lesson" started.

I was listening to the radio one day not long after my arrival when two guards came to my cell and barked out, "shake down!" they began knocking my things on the floor and walking on them, deliberately trying to destroy what little property I was allowed. One of the guards pulled a knife blade out of his boot and tossed it on my bunk, than called for a camera. He took a picture of the knife and wrote a report saying he found it in my cell. I couldn't believe what I was seeing. I thought being set-up for things I didn't do would stop once I got to prison. I was wrong.

They threw me in "the hole." The hole is a group of cells located at the back of the prison, out of sight and hearing of everyone else. Temperatures can reach nearly 120 degrees in the summer, and it's even darker and filthier than the rest of the prison. You aren't allowed to have anything when you're in the hole—no toothbrush, no comb, no deodorant, and no contact with the outside world. Its purpose is complete and absolute sensory deprivation. You spend thirty days in the hole, no matter what your offense is. Beating someone half to death or making a homemade lamp shade to go over your light both carry the same penalty: thirty days in the hole. The only thing that differs is how you're treated while you're back there.

While in the hole I was beaten, starved, spit on, threatened with death, and subject to various other forms of abuse, both large and small, all at the hands of guards. The reason? The warden said I made the ADC look bad in the interviews I was doing. One night at almost twelve o'clock I heard keys jingling in the hallway and knew they were coming for me. Two guards came into my cell, handcuffed me, and took me up to the warden's office. One guard held me up by the hair as the warden choked me. I could smell the alcohol on his breath as he ranted and raved about how "sick" I was. One of the guards kept punching me in the stomach while repeatedly asking, "Are you going to tell anyone about this? Are you?" I had never been subjected to anything like that in my life. I thought adults were only that barbaric in movies.

It happened more than once. On three more occasions, guards came into my cell and beat me. Once I was chained to the bars of the cell while three of them took turns. Another time it was five of them. I was told that they planned on keeping me in the hole for a very long time. Every time the thirty days were up, they could just give me another thirty for something else. The only thing that saved me was the way word leaked out into the rest of the prison, and a deacon from the Catholic Church heard about it. He told the warden that if it didn't stop he would start telling people what was going on. They didn't want to risk it, so I was taken out of the hole and put back into the barracks with the rest of death row.

The thing about the prison administration is that they will abuse you as long as you're quiet. The only way they can't hurt you is if someone is paying attention. I started talking to more people, doing more interviews, because I knew only that would make them leave me alone. They can't afford to harm you if the world is watching. They could not drag me into a dark alley, if I had a spotlight shining on me. I even filed a lawsuit against the warden and some of the guards responsible.

In the end it was a waste of my time, as they once again chose the attorney who represented me for the suit. I only saw him once, about ten minutes before the "trial" began. He didn't do one single thing to help me. I was refused the right to a trial in front of a jury, and he just shrugged his shoulders as if to say "Oh, well. That's life." Instead, a judge alone decided my case. I wasn't even allowed to talk during the proceeding. We didn't go to a courtroom, the judge came to the prison so the session could be held in a small room out of public view. The lies the administration told were pretty incredible. They "proved" that the warden couldn't have done anything to me, because he was in the hospital recovering from a heart attack. Did the lawyer they appointed me investigate these claims? No. He sat quietly drinking a soda.

In the end, it all worked out. The warden was fired, although it wasn't because of anything he'd done to me. Some of his other foul deeds caught up to him. The worst of the guards were also either fired or given promotions and shipped to other prisons in the state. The one who put the knife in my cell continued to work there for many more years, despite constant reports of abuse. Eventually the ADC had no choice but to "take action" against him—he was caught on camera beating a handcuffed inmate in the face. No charges were ever filed against any of these people. After all, it's not like they were actually abusing people, you know. They're just prisoners.

◆   ◆   ◆

I was still a child when I was sent here. I grew into adulthood, both mentally and physically, in this hellhole. I came into this situation wide-eyed and naïve. Now I view most everything and everyone with narrow eyed suspicion. I've learned the hard way that the world is not my friend. I thought that pretty much the entire human race wanted me to die a slow, painful death, until a miracle occurred. It seems my hopes of receiving divine intervention weren't completely misplaced.

While in jail I had granted an interview to a crew from HBO. They wanted to film a documentary. I had mostly forgotten about it after I had been in prison for a year or so, thinking nothing had come of it. They had interviewed me, Domini, my family, the cops, the victim's families, and anyone else who would talk. They also filmed the entire trial, from beginning to end. I didn't see it when it finally aired, but many other people around the world did. Contrary to popular reckoning, not everyone in prison has cable television. I personally do not know of any who do.

On a daily basis I started receiving letters and cards from people all over the country who had seen the film and were horrified by it. The overwhelming sentiment was, "That could have been me they did that to!" You have to understand that up until this point I had received no sympathy or empathy from anyone. Everywhere I turned I found nothing but disgust, contempt, and hatred. The whole world wanted me to die. It's impossible to have any hope in the face of such opposition. Now I was suddenly receiving letters from people saying, 'I'm so sorry for what had been done to you, I wish there was something I could do to help."

A single letter like this would have been enough to kindle a tiny spark of hope in my heart, but I received hundreds. Every day at least one or two arrived, sometimes as many as ten or twenty. I would lie on my bunk and flip through these letters over and over again, savoring them like a fat kid with a fistful of candy. Sometimes tears streamed from my eyes as I looked to the heavens and whispered "Thank you, thank you," over and over again. I clutched those letters to my chest and slept with them under my head. I had never been so thankful for anything in my entire life.

One thing I've noticed time and time again in prison is how quickly people in the outside world forget you. Their lives do not stop simply because yours does. Sooner or later they get over the grieving process and move on. Even your family. Two years is a very long time for someone to stick by your side once you're in prison. Most don't even last that long. Domini moved on with her life, she's now married, has a beautiful daughter, and lives all the way on the other side of the country. I haven't even seen my own father in many, many years. He and my mother divorced and both remarried. He has another family to worry about and care for now. There's not much he could have done for me anyway. All around me are people who have been abandoned to their fates. No one comes to see them or offers encouragement. No one writes them long letters with news from home. They have no one to call when they're so sad or scared that they feel they can't go on. No one sends them a few dollars so they don't have to eat the rancid prison food. They are the true living dead. The world has moved on, and they are forgotten.

The thought that I could have so easily been one of them fills my heart with terror. I'm fortunate beyond my ability to describe because I've had a few friends who have stuck by my side since almost the beginning.

Three devoted characters from the west coast came into my life years ago, and have been a constant source of support ever since. Kathy, Grove, and Burk. Collectively they are "the K.G.B." These people have gone above and beyond the call of duty to do everything they can to help. They've invested countless hours of their own time to spreading the word about this case. They never miss a court hearing and never forget a birthday. Through their unwavering belief and devotion many others have come to hear about and join the crusade. There are now more names than I can mention, and I could write a "Thank you" book consisting of nothing but names of people who have went out of their way to help. Kathy, Grove, and Burk, along with the assistance of a fourth California angel named Lisa have donated their time and energy to maintaining a tremendous Web site on which the general public can now read every scrap of information that exists about the case. Seeing that justice is done has become the focus of their existence, but they also do what they can to make my life a little easier. They encourage people to write, just so I know I've not been forgotten. Another friend, Jené, maintains a "wish list" of books on the site, which hundreds of people have sent to me. Things have come a long way since the trial. I no longer feel like the most reviled creature on earth. Some days I can now make myself believe that the entire world doesn't view me as a stain on the underwear of society. When the filmmakers released a second documentary things picked up even more. My record so far has been receiving 188 letters in a single day. Once you know what it means to be hated the way I have been, it teaches you to appreciate those tokens of love even more.

XXXII

I am a Sagittarius, a fire sign. Sagittarians are known for their need to keep moving, exploring, learning. Much like fire, it must be fed or it will die. What it must be fed is a constant stream of new experiences. There aren't many journeys to be undertaken when locked in a cage. Outward motion comes to a complete standstill. You have two choices: turn inwards and start your journey there, or go insane.

One of the first things that both Ju San/Frankie and Gene told me was that you must turn your cell into a school and monastery. You will spend twenty-three hours a day in that cell, all alone. Most people can't take being forced to come face to face with themselves, so they become loud and mean, like baboons looking for a shiny object to distract themselves. The number one distraction is television. Most people in prison grow fat and out of shape as they spend endless hours in front of the T.V. They'll watch football, basketball, baseball, soap operas, the Jerry Springer show, Judge Judy, and anything else that crosses the screen. They watch it from the moment they get up in the morning until the moment they go back to bed. If I didn't want to become a brain dead, shuffling, obese Neanderthal, then I had to nip it in the bud and not allow myself to fall into the pattern.

I moved from one area of study to another. In addition to the Theosophy texts from gene and the Buddhists texts from Ju San, I began practicing a kind of Christian Mysticism called *A Course in Miracles*. I was introduced to this school of thought by a gentleman named Mike.

I never could figure out if the guy was a genius or a psychopath. He wasn't actually on death row, but he was what is known as a "porter." He was doing a life without parole sentence, and his job was to keep death row clean. Sweep, mop, wash windows, scrub the showers, dust, etc. Those were his jobs. I awoke one morning at two AM because of a scritch-scritch-scritching noise. Getting up to see what it was, I saw Mike on his hands and knees scrubbing the floor with a toothbrush. When I asked him exactly what in the hell he was doing, he explained that he no longer needed sleep so he figured he might as well use his time constructively. That was a typical Mike answer. He said only the ego needs sleep. He was also prone to have visions. He once told me he was shown that if he fasted for a week, he could reward himself with an ice cream (If someone sends you money, the prison has a small list of things you can buy. Ice cream is one of them). Just when you were positive he was insane he did something to stop you dead in your tracks with wonder.

A Course in Miracles is a book of practices that takes you a year to complete if you follow each lesson. Its aim is to completely change the way your mind has been programmed to think since birth. You come to experience reality in an entirely different manner, in which anything is possible. It's based on quantum physics, but uses biblical terminology. It's become rather popular in recent years, and there are now study groups devoted to A Course in Miracles all over the country.

Mike hung out in front of my cell every day, sitting on a five-gallon bucket. Our only topic of conversation was A Course in Miracles and how it related to The Holy Kabbalah, a book of Jewish mysticism. The Kabbalah is what we dedicated our time to learning about after finishing Miracles. Mike was learning from a guy in general population who was a Kabbalist, then he came and explained things to me. I was amazed at how many students of various forms of mysticism you find in prison. They're usually determined to make the most of their time and to not repeat the same mistakes. These are men starving for a kind of knowledge not given in the mundane world, ready to learn and pass on what they already know. I continued my study alone after Mike was sent to another part of the prison.

Next I went on to learn about the philosophy and practice of an organization known as "The Golden Dawn." This was a group of people who practiced metaphysical rites of passage to mark the different stages in the evolution of consciousness. It was all about the constant learning and growth process that everyone goes through, and how to speed it up. The great poet W.B. Yeats was one of the more well-known students of this school of thought. I had my nose in these books morning, noon, and night.

Many people donated money to a college fund that was set up for Jason and I, so I began taking courses from a local college here in Arkansas. At first, I was interested mostly in psychology, but mixed a few other things in, such a sociology and reading German, for good measure. Psychology seemed infinitely interesting to me, with all of its experiments and nature versus nurture debates. Perhaps that's because of the environment in which I live. The vast majority of the death row population is either mentally ill or mentally retarded, and I've always thought it good to know as much as possible about the world that surrounds you.

I later realized psychology was not my love at all—it was history. I've grown to love history more than any other subject, and have come to believe you can understand far more about the world through history than you can through psychology, especially if it's military history. At first I delved into every aspect and every era of history, but gradually my scope narrowed as I began to realize what I was more drawn to.

My love is Italian history, specifically the cities of Florence and Venice, from the time period between 1400 and 1800. My role model is Cosimo di Medici, though I also like Lorenzo the Magnificent. What I love about that period in time is the social structure and all the intrigue that accompanied it. Among aristocratic circles life was like a chess game. You had to weigh your every word, as the conversation was filled with subtlety. Social success or failure could hinge on whom you were seen making eye contact with. Not to mention the decadent styles and fashions that were all the rage. No one was wearing baggy jeans and backwards baseball caps. These days no one makes an effort. Fashion and style are things I pay a great deal of attention to now, probably because I haven't been able to put on real clothes in eleven years. Sometimes I think I'd give anything to be able to wear a suit and tie. That's all I want to wear. I drool over Brooks Brother's ads. When I watch the World news I pay as much attention to what tie Peter Jennings is wearing as I do to the top stories. Snappy dresser, that guy. You'd never catch him in jeans and tennis shoes.

◆　　　◆　　　◆

When it comes to education and life lessons, the two things I've learned the most from are my wife and my Zen training. What wife is that, you ask? Well, first things first, eager reader. It's easier to explain things one step at a time.

I've lost count of how many executions have taken place during my time here. Somewhere between twenty-five and thirty, I believe. Some of those men I knew well and was close to. Others, I couldn't stand the sight of. Still, I wasn't happy to see any of them go the way they did. It's a fate I'd wish on no one.

Many people rallied to Ju San's cause, begging the state to spare his life, but in the end it did no good. He had committed such a heinous crime. Frankie Parker had been a brutal heroin addict who held a police station hostage. Over the years he had become Ju San—an ordained Rinzai Zen Buddhist priest with many friends and supporters. On the night of his execution, shortly after he was pronounced dead, his teacher and spiritual advisor was allowed to walk down death row and greet the inmates.

I was watching the news coverage of Ju San's death when someone stepped in front of my door. I turned to see a little old bald man in a black robe and sandals, clutching a strand of prayer beads. He had wild white eyebrows that were so out of control they looked like small horns. He practically had handlebar mustaches above his eyes. He seemed intense and concentrated as he introduced himself. A lot of Protestant preachers come through death row, but they all seemed to think themselves better than us. You could tell it by the way most of them didn't even bother to shake hands. Kobutsu (that was his name) wasn't like that at all. He made direct, unwavering eye contact and seemed to be genuinely pleased to be meeting me. It had been his personal mission to do everything he could to help Ju San, and was pretty torn up over the execution. Before he left he said I should feel free to write to him at any time. I took him up on that offer. That was quite a few years ago, though I still hear from him from time to time. He's not doing so well health-wise these days.

He and I began corresponding, and I eventually made a formal request of him that he become my teacher. He accepted. Kobutsu is an incredibly odd character. Imagine a Zen monk who chain smokes, tells jokes that could be described as pornographic, and always has an appreciative leer for the female anatomy—then you begin to see the paradox that is Kobutsu. Holy man, carnival barker, anarchist, artist, friend, and asshole all rolled up in one robe. He is totally unpredictable; you never know what outrageous bullshit would come from his mouth next. I immediately took a shine to him.

He sent me books about the old Zen masters, different Buddhist practices, and small cards to make shrines out of. He retuned not long after Ju San's execution to perform a Refuge ceremony for another death row inmate, and I was allowed to participate in the ceremony. Refuge is the Buddhist equivalent of baptism. It's like declaring your intention to follow this path, so that the world witnesses it. It was a beautiful ceremony that stirred something in my heart. I was glad to have been a part of it.

I turned to Zen out of desperation. I had been through hell, traumatized, and sent to death row for a crime I did not commit. There's a lot of anger that comes with experiences like that. In fact my anger and outrage were eating me alive. Hatred was growing in my heart because of the way I was being treated on a daily basis.

In the movies it was always the other prisoners you had to watch out for. In real life it was the guards and the administration. They went out of their way to make my life harder and more stressful than it already was, as if being on death row in itself were not enough. They could take a man sent to prison for writing bad checks and torment him until he becomes a violent offender. I didn't want these people to be able to change me, to touch me inside and turn me as rotten and stagnant as them. I turned to Zen for help.

Under Kobutsu's tutelage I began sitting zazen mediation on a daily basis. At first it was agony to have to sit still and stare at the floor for fifteen minutes. Over time I became more accustomed to it, and managed to increase my sitting time to twenty minutes a day. I put away all reading material except for Zen texts and meditation manuals. I'd read nothing else for the next three years.

About six months after the other prisoner's ceremony, Kobutsu returned to perform it for me. I can't describe the magick this ritual held for me. It increased my determination to practice tenfold. I was walking on air, happy for weeks afterwards. I started every day with a smile on my face and not even the guards got to me. I think it was a little unsettling to them to strip search a man who smiles at you through the whole ordeal.

Kobutsu and I continued to correspond through letters and also talked on the phone. His conversations were a mixture of encouragement, instruction, nasty jokes, and bizarre tales of his latest adventures. I began to seriously contemplate the possibility that he may very well be insane, but you can't argue with results. Through constant daily practice, my life was definitely improving. I even constructed a small shrine of paper Buddhas in my cell to give me inspiration. I was now sitting zazen meditation for two hours a day and still pushing myself. I'd not yet had that elusive enlightenment experience that I'd heard so much about, and I desperately wanted it.

One year after I had taken Refuge, Kobutsu decided it was time for my Jukai ceremony. Jukai is lay ordination, where one begins to take vows. It's also where you are renamed, to symbolize taking on a new life and shedding the old one. Only the teacher decides when you are ready to receive Jukai.

My ceremony was going to be extra special, as Kobutsu himself would not be performing it. Instead it was performed by Shodo Harada-Xoshi, one of the greatest living Zen Masters on earth. He was the abbot of a beautiful temple in Japan, and flew to Arkansas for this occasion. I anticipated the event for weeks beforehand, so much that I had trouble sleeping at night. The morning of the big event I was up before dawn, shaving my head and preparing to meet the master.

All morning I jerked to attention and crane my neck to get a better look every time the door to our barracks opened, thinking perhaps my guests had arrived. When they walked in just before lunch it created a stir among the inmates. A low buzz of conversation erupted, people asking each other "Who's that? What's going on?"

Kobutsu was first in line through the door. I could see the light reflecting off of his freshly shaved, pink head. I also noticed he had abandoned his usual Japanese sandals in favor of a pair of high-top converse tennis shoes. To see a pair of sneakers protruding from under the hem of a monk's robe is an odd contrast. Behind him walked Harada-Roshi. He wore the same style robe as Kobutsu, only in pristine condition. Kobutsu tended to have the occasional mustard stain on his, and didn't seem to mind one bit.

Harada-Roshi was small and thin, but had a very commanding presence. Despite his warm smile there was something about him that was very formal in an almost military sort of way. I believe the first word that came to mind when I saw him was discipline. He seemed disciplined beyond anything a human could achieve, and it greatly inspired me. To this day I still strive to have as much discipline about myself as Harada-Roshi. Beneath his warmth and friendliness was a will of solid steel.

Following Harada-Roshi was Chisan, a female priest from the Japanese temple. I had never seen a female priest in person before. I might not have even known she was female until I looked closely, because she wore the same black robe, and her head was shaved just as bald as the rest of us. She was Harada-Roshi's translator, as the only word he could speak in English was "Hello." She was filled with good humor and extremely fun to be around. After the ceremony she told me, "Now I am your big sister, and you must do as I say!" As I tried to judge how serious this warning was, she erupted into peals of laughter.

Last in line was Kobutsu's new lady friend, Dakota. She stood out from everyone else just because she had long, blond hair and was wearing jeans. Many people think all monks are celibate. This isn't true of the Japanese Rinzai tradition, where monks often marry and have children.

We were all lead into a tiny room that served as death row's chapel. After everyone greeted each other and gave "hello" hugs, we all settled into our seats. Harada-Roshi talked about the difference in Japan and America, about his temple back home, and about how few Asians came to learn at the old temple now, it was mostly Americans who wanted to learn. His voice was low, raspy, and rapid fire. Japanese isn't usually described as a beautiful language, but I was entranced by it. I dearly wished I could make such poetic elegant sounding words come from my own mouth.

Harada-Roshi set up a small travel-altar to perform the ceremony. The altar cloth was white silk, and on it was a small Buddha statue, a canvas covered with calligraphy, and an incense burner. We all dropped a pinch of the exotic smelling incense into the burner as an offering, and then opened our Sutra books to begin the proper chants. Kobutsu had to help me turn the pages of my book because the guards made me wear chains on my hands and feet. During the ceremony I was given the name Koson. I loved that name and all it symbolized, and scribbled it everywhere. I was also presented with my *rakusu*.

A rakusu is made of black cloth, and is suspended from your neck. It covers your *hara*, which is the energy center about two finger widths below your belly button. It has two black, cloth straps and a wooden ring/buckle. It's sewn in a pattern similar to the way a rice paddy would look if viewed from the air. It represents the Buddha's robe. This is the only part of my robe the administration allowed me to keep inside the prison. On the inside of it Harada-Roshi had painted beautiful calligraphy characters which said, "Great effort, without fail, brings great light." It was my most prized possession until one day years later the prison guards took it from me.

The canvas on the altar was also given to me. It translates to "Moonbeams pierce to the bottom of the pools, yet in the water not a trace remains." I proudly put it on display in my cell.

Kobutsu wrote a wonderful article about the experience, and it was printed in a Buddhist magazine called *The Shambala Sun*, along with lots of pictures of us all posing together. They printed a small piece I had written as a sidebar. I must have looked at that article and pictures a thousand times over the years. Just looking at it gives me strength to continue.

◆   ◆   ◆

I ventured into the realm of Zen to gain a handle on my negative emotional states, which I had achieved to a great extent, but I now approached my practice in a much more aggressive manner. Much like weight lifting, I continued to pile it on. On weekends I was now sitting zazen meditation for five hours a day. My prayer beads were always in my hand as I constantly chanted mantras. I practiced hatha yoga for at least an hour a day. I became a vegetarian. Still, I did not have a breakthrough *Kensho* experience. Kensho is a moment in which you see reality with crystal clear vision, what a lot of people refer to as "enlightenment." I didn't voice my thoughts out loud, but I was beginning to harbor strong suspicions that it was nothing more than a myth.

A teacher of Tibetan Buddhism started coming to the prison once a week to instruct anyone interested. I attended these sessions, which were specifically tailored to be of use to those on death row. One practice I and another inmate were taught is called *phowa*. It consists of pushing your energy out through the top of your head at the moment of death. It still did not bring about that life changing moment I was in search of.

◆   ◆   ◆

There is a man named Bob who lives in Tennessee and pours concrete for a living. He's also written two books on the subject of meditation and mystical experiences. He was once a Zen teacher but decided to hang up his robes one day for a more mundane life. He had taken his own experiences and stripped them of all religious connotations and terminology so that it was more practical and useful to the average person. The name he gave his technique was "non-conceptual awareness." If you passed Bob on the street you would never look at him twice. He was average in every way; he certainly didn't look like anyone you would prostrate yourself at the feet of. You would never guess that Bob had had that experience I was now desperate to have, but inside that plain, average body was an incredible mind, and I consider it a miracle to have found him. Who would believe that an enlightened Zen master lived in Tennessee and poured concrete for a living? Not I, simply because he didn't look exotic enough to play the part.

This southern-fried guru became a friend of mine, and I will forever be grateful to him. I once wrote him a letter discussing technical aspects of Zen teachings, one of the key points being emptiness. Zen teaches that we really do not exist, and I just couldn't buy that. How could I not exist if I can reach down and touch myself? This not existing, which is what is called the emptiness teaching, was really disturbing me. I wrote to Bob and said, "If I don't exist then why does it hurt if I hit my hand with a hammer?" His answer, which changed me forever, was, "No one said the pain is not real. No one said the body is not real. It's the entity you believe experiences the pain that is not real."

It was as if those words broke a dam in me. All the meditation, all the studying, all the sutras, all the yoga—it had filled me to the bursting point, and now it all overflowed. The only thing that makes that description inadequate is that there was no "me" behind the experience. It seemed to expand and deepen constantly over the course of the next year. There was only the experience itself, there was no one to experience it.

To give a more concrete and easily understandable experience I'll use daily chores as an example. When I brushed my teeth the act of brushing occurred, and it was perceived by pure consciousness, but I no longer lived under the delusion that there was an entity called "Damien" to do it.

Many people have told me this is a horrifying concept, and that they would never want to cease to exist. That's the illusion. The truth is that we never existed in the first place, and only made the mistake of thinking our reflection was who we really are. All of my anger and outrage slipped away. Nothing anyone did, even the prison guards, could get to me. I could see myself in everyone. It was like every man, woman, and child on earth were fingers on the same hand, but had forgotten it. There are no words capable of expressing how simple everything was, and how beautiful, but I still wanted to try to explain it. I wanted everyone to be able to see the world the way I now did, so I grabbed a pen and began writing. The result, which I finished in less than a month, was a group of essays that covered topics from Alchemy and sex, to meditation and enlightenment. I called them collectively *Little Essays Towards Truth*, in honor of one of my favorite historical spiritual seekers.

For some people the experience I had only lasts a split second. For others it lasts their entire life. I consciously and deliberately discarded it, so I could move on to the next thing. I didn't want a "holy" life of prayer and contemplation. I want a life of strife, lust, striving, seeking, struggling, and debauchery. I was not content to settle for one experience when there are a whole lifetime of experiences to be had. I am so hungry for knowledge that I live several lives at once to acquire it. A Catholic, a Buddhist, a reader and a writer, a sinner, a philosopher, a husband and a father, a native American and a white man. I no longer have any desire to fit into any category. I see no reason why I can't love pornography and the art of Michelangelo equally. I want to see life from every angle.

I feel as if I've learned a tremendous amount from my excursion into the realm of eastern thought, philosophy and practice, things I'll carry with me to the end of my days. Still, it doesn't come close to the lessons learned from and with the woman who is now my wife.

XXXIII

In certain tribal cultures spirit guides were represented by animals. The animal guides usher people into the next realm of development in their lives. In plain language, they make us grow as a person. My guide to growth is a beautiful monkey.

My wife is the single most erotic and intelligent creature that has ever existed. She can have all the poise and grace of a feline, but shining from her eyes is pure monkey mischief. She is my strength and my heart. Without her to keep me going I would have withered and died long ago. I have no reason to keep breathing, outside of her. She is my life. I had been on death row for about two years when I received an odd letter in the mail. It was from a woman who was obsessed with movies, and had recently seen a documentary about my case in a small art house type theater in Brooklyn, New York. She did something no one else had ever done; she apologized for invading my privacy by seeking me out. That really struck me, because I felt like I no longer had any privacy. My entire life had been exposed for anyone and everyone to come examine and poke at with a stick. I was a fly that had its wings ripped off by an obnoxious fat kid. I was the proverbial ant under the magnifying glass. Every day I received letters from people who did nothing but ask questions about the most intimate aspects of my life, almost as if the world was entitled to demand anything of me they wanted to know. Imagine being hounded by the paparazzi, only instead of taking your picture they throw rocks and try to dissect you.

So, this was a woman who understood the value of common courtesy. She said she felt horrible about what I'd been through and was compelled to contact me, but that she didn't want to intrude. I immediately wrote back to her, and ever since that day we've tried to write each other every single day for the past eight years. Our letters to each other now fill up a closet.

She's the most magickal thing on earth, but it took me at least a year to be able to understand her, because she was so foreign to anything I'd ever known. She was from New York, college educated, a world traveler who's been from South America to the Middle East, and an architect who had worked on projects for people I'd only heard of from Hollywood movies. I was introduced to a whole new way of life through her.

It was a slow and gradual process, forging a world together. In the beginning I couldn't have even articulated what we were doing because I had no concept of subtlety. Now it's a personal obsession of mine, to know more of subtlety. I believe it started with literature, like the Latin American writer Julio Cortazar.

His writing had had a huge impact on her life and his books were among her most valued possessions. When she sent them to me I was dumbfounded. I truly couldn't understand why anyone had thought these stories important enough to commit to paper. They made no sense to me. I had been raised to believe a real story had a beginning, a middle, and a conclusion in which the loose ends were tied up. Therefore the stories I received from her seemed to defy logic. Ah, but those books were the least of my headaches.

Her music and movies baffled me a thousand times more so. Before me, her life was movies. Not big Hollywood productions designed to entertain popcorn munching morons, but foreign films, art house movies, independent productions, etc. Everything I considered a waste of film, in other words. There was no way I would pay to see any movie that didn't have monsters in it. My motto was "No vampire, no werewolf, no zombie—no ticket."

I knew I was in love with her when I started to wake up in the middle of the night furious and cursing her for making me feel the way she did. It was pain beyond belief. Nothing has ever hurt me that way. I tried to sleep as much as possible just to escape. I was grinding my teeth down to nubs. Now, years later, it's exactly the opposite. Now there is no pain, yet she still makes my heart explode with incredible bursts of love. Now there is only fun and love and silliness. She drives me to frenzy, because I can never get enough.

She had to fly from New York to Arkansas every time we saw each other, so in addition to the phone bill this was an extremely expensive relationship. She always laughs now when she tells anyone about the first time I ever called her. She picked up the phone to hear a deep, southern accent ask, "Are you okay?" It was such a shock to her system that it took a second for her to think of a reply. She said it nearly killed her. Now, eight years later, she still sometimes teases me about my accent, but her friends in New York often tell her that she is starting to sound just like me.

For the first three years that we were together we couldn't even touch each other. When she came to see me there was a sheet of glass separating us. It was maddening, and we often blew through the screen at the bottom of the glass just to be able to feel each other's breath. I loved to sit and look at her, as she has an absolutely perfect body. It's every man's fantasy—like a 1950s pin-up model. To have such intelligence in a body like that is a miracle. She takes exquisite care of herself, and it shows. At the age of forty she looks like she's in her mid twenties. It inspires me, makes me always try harder to be better for her. She says I know everything, and is always amazed by the information I can supply on any topic she thinks of. The thing is, I do it just the dazzle her. I devour books by the boxful, just to impress her with what I know. I exercise twice a day—push ups, sit ups, jumping jacks, running in place, and yoga—just so she'll be as enamored with my body as I am of hers.

We finally got to touch each other for the first time in December of 1999, when we were married. So far we've had the first and only Buddhist wedding ceremony in the history of the Arkansas prison system. The guards had no idea what to make of it. It was a small ceremony that lasted about forty-five minutes, and we were allowed to have six friends there to witness it. Afterwards people said it was so beautiful that they forgot it was taking place in a prison. At one point I broke out in a cold sweat and nearly fainted, just because that's every man's genetic predisposition to weddings.

Lorri (that's her name, by the way) now lives in Arkansas. She moved here to start a whole new life and be with me. She is to me what Sharon is to Ozzy. She keeps every aspect of my life neatly filed and managed, even when I rebel against it. She now represents me to the world at large. When she sits in at a meeting everyone has learned that it's the same as if I were sitting there. She is the only person I've ever trusted to take care of me as if she's taking care of herself. When things need to be done "out there," I can rest easy knowing she will tend to it.

I spend every day of the week looking forward to Friday, when we have our weekly picnic. Everything else is just a countdown to those three hours. We don't spend all our time waiting on some distant day when I'm out of prison, because we have a life together right here and now. This is our life, and there is not a moment that we're not in each other's minds and hearts.

Her parents are both extremely supportive of our relationship and make trips to the prison for occasional visits. They've been a hell of a lot more accepting than I would have been if I had a daughter and she announced that she'd married a guy on death row. My son loves her as well, and she gets to take on the role of stepmother whenever he comes for a visit. She's better suited to the part of parent than I, because I've still not gotten used to someone addressing me as "Dad."

I would gladly go through everything I've been through again if I knew that's what it took for Lorri to find me. She found me when I was drowning and breathed life into me. I had given up and she instilled me with hope. For the first time in my life, I am whole.

◆   ◆   ◆

I'm guessing that brings me to the present. I'm now at the same prison as Jason and Jesse Misskelley, although we can't see each other or communicate. I found my way here a little less than a year ago, when I was awakened at two A.M. by a group of madcap funsters with M-16 assault rifles and attack dogs. They roused all thirty-seven of us up, wrapped us in chains, and packed us into vans like sardines. There were eight prisoners and two guards in each van. It was a tight fit and a long, uncomfortable ride.

Once we arrived here we were placed in what amounts to solitary confinement. It's a concrete cell with a solid steel door. We never come in contact with other inmates, and you can only talk to the person next to you by pressing your face into a crack and screaming. It's pretty filthy, as we've been here for almost a year now and my floor hasn't been swept or mopped once in that time. They clean outside the cells if an inspection is coming, but never inside. I haven't felt sunlight on my skin in over nine months. It took a while to adjust to the constant confinement and isolation, but I don't even mind it now. You have a hell of a lot more privacy, which can be a rare commodity in prison.

My first two appeals were turned down by the Arkansas court system. Big surprise there, eh? I'm now preparing to enter federal court, but at least now I have competent attorneys, due in large part to Eddie Vedder. Eddie has shown himself to be a true friend time and time again. How many rock stars do you know that visit guys in prison when they come through town? It's always a tremendous amount of fun whenever he stops by and tells of his latest adventures.

I've also got my fingers crossed right now, hoping the results of a DNA test come back soon. It seems to take forever sometimes. DNA testing has come quite a ways in the eleven years I've been locked up. They can do things now that they couldn't do a decade ago. There was no way to do it until now because no one could afford it. The difference now is a one man army named Henry Rollins who has worked his ass off to make sure it happens.

I'm still stunned every time I see a letter arrive in the mail with a return address for "H. Rollins," because it hits me that I'm trading correspondence with a living legend. He's determined to see the truth come out, and nothing stops him once he's made his mind up about getting something done.

It's things like that, which really let me know how far this case has come. Still, I'd be lying if I said I wasn't scared sometimes. Every once in a while I'm damn near petrified, but I have no choice but to struggle on.

XXXIV

Recent events in my life include being adopted (again) and catching a glimpse of Jason. The adoption was completed just last week. At thirty years of age I was still parent shopping. Cally, also known as "Mama Muse," decided she was no longer content with a houseful of cats ad decided to adopt me despite my constant sarcasm. The nastier I am, the more she brags to all her friends about me. This is a woman who has pictures of barnyard animals on her socks and listens in to every conversation around her in the coffee house. She insists on sending me progress reports on the health of her ninety-nine cats, including which ones have diarrhea.

Her job is to help shape the minds of today's youth by giving advice at a school in California. And people wonder how Californians gained the reputation of being fruitcakes. I point the finger of blame at Cally. You know she can't be normal—she voluntarily chose to adopt me, after all.

The Jason sighting took place on a Friday afternoon while Lorri and I were in the midst of our weekly picnic. I looked up to see him about thirty feet away in the hallway, looking at me through the glass. He raised his hand and smiled, then he was gone, like a ghost. I wish I could have talked to him, if only to say, "Just hang on." That's the same thing I keep telling myself.

Just hang on.

Damien Echols
5/22/04
9:38 P.M.

978-0-595-35701-7
0-595-35701-6